*f*P

Peter Walsh

ENOUGH ALREADY!

Clearing Mental Clutter to Become the Best You

FREE PRESS

New York   London   Toronto   Sydney

Free Press
A Division of Simon & Schuster, Inc.
1230 Avenue of the Americas
New York, NY 10020

First Free Press hardcover edition February 2009

FREE PRESS and colophon are trademarks of Simon & Schuster, Inc.

For information about special discounts for bulk purchases,
please contact Simon & Schuster Special Sales at
1-800-456-6798 or business@simonandschuster.com

Designed by Katy Riegel

Manufactured in the United States of America

10   9   8   7   6   5   4   3   2   1

Library of Congress Cataloging-in-Publication Data
Walsh, Peter.
    Enough already! : clearing mental clutter to become the best you / Peter Walsh with
Hilary Liftin.
        p.   cm.
Includes index.
1. Simplicity.   2. Orderliness.   I. Title.
BJ1496.W35   2008
646.7—dc22   2008029499

ISBN-13: 978-1-4165-6018-0
ISBN-10:   1-4165-6018-1

To my mother
Agnes Catherine Kelleher Walsh,
who, with seven children,
invented the phrase "Enough Already!"

Contents

Contents

Barn's burnt down—
now
I can see the moon.

Masahide (1657–1723)

Introduction

Dealing with clutter is my job. Helping people dig out from under the overwhelming mess that fills their homes is part of my daily routine. To the amazement of many, I love what I do. Hundreds and hundreds of families have had me into their homes to tackle clutter. Hundreds of thousands of others have seen me on TV and cleared their own spaces using the same techniques that have worked so well for me. But I have a little secret that I have waited a while to let you in on. Those massive piles of clutter are only the tip of the iceberg. While the clutter you see around you might seem bad, even overwhelming and paralyzing, the physical clutter that fills our homes is nothing compared to the invisible clutter that fills our heads.

Consider this: If you can lose your car keys in your own home, or if it takes you half an hour to find your checkbook, or if you have ever tripped and fallen over your own belongings, then imagine what the clutter in your head is doing to you. In theory, you can see the clutter that you have to climb over every day, but in reality you get so used to walking around it that you can forget it's actually there. Somehow, it becomes invisible—at least to you. The clutter in your head is even more difficult to deal with because you truly can't see it and neither can anyone else. Over time, you come to accept the way you are as the way you will be forever. I'm here to tell you that it doesn't have to be so.

As the "organization guy" I have met and received e-mails from thousands—maybe tens of thousands—of people who are overwhelmed by clutter. Collectibles, furniture, paper, clothes, books, toys, and shoes fill up the spaces in their homes where they should be living their lives. Where does all this stuff come from? How is it that seemingly reasonable, honest, hard-working people—people who might be your friends, colleagues, relatives, or YOU—find themselves nearly buried alive? We buy so much stuff and we fill every corner of our homes with it. But it's not only the stuff that's the problem. Sure—we buy "the stuff," but we also invest in what I call "the promise." We buy exercise machines, but we are really investing in the promise of flat abs. We buy clothing, but we are really investing in the promise of being more attractive. We buy all that stuff from late-night infomercials, but we are really investing in the idea that somehow our lives will be better and our homes will be happier. It just doesn't work like that. I know, because I have waded through homes choking with more stuff than you can imagine. Homes overwhelmed with stuff and lives littered with the empty promises that the stuff didn't fulfill.

We buy all that stuff because we think it will make us happy. We think that if we collect all the right things—the right home, the right clothes, the right electronics, the right cars, the right appliances—we will eventually accumulate the life we imagine for ourselves. In buying what we want, we hope to acquire the life we desire. If the primary relationship in your life is with your stuff, what you'll eventually find is that it's not a give-and-take relationship. Stuff can be a real bitch! It's very demanding. It fills space. It costs money. It doesn't respond to your changing needs. It promises everything, delivers nothing, and eventually just stresses you out. Chasing the life you want by accumulating more stuff is a dead-end street.

People are always surprised when they realize that the real challenge in decluttering and getting organized has little to do—at least initially—with their stuff. The real challenge isn't wading through their belongings, although this has to be done. The real challenge is the question that comes before we tackle anything in their home. The first, most challenging task that I give the people I work with is to speak about the vision they have for their lives. Without understanding what this vision looks like, none of the work that I (or you) do can be successful or sustained. Start with the stuff (as most people are inclined to do when they try to conquer their clutter) and you are pretty much guaranteed failure. Start with the vision you have for the life you want and you have taken the first real step to long-term and remarkable change.

The letters that appear throughout this book are a sampling of the many e-mails and notes that I receive every day. I've removed names and identifying details, but the sentiments are genuine and the people who have expressed them are real. In addition, the anecdotes in the book about other people are used to illustrate common problems I've encountered in my life and work, but they do not include real names or identifying details.

Dear Peter:
I'm stuck in a self-defeating rut. I know it. I'm even pretty sure I know why I can't take the necessary action to get out of it—

even by doing nothing, the rut keeps getting deeper. The reason I can't motivate myself to lose weight, clean the house, or get involved in anything is always the same: FEAR. Fear of coming out of the safe hiding place I've created. As long as the house is a mess, I don't have to worry about inviting anyone over; as long as I'm overweight, I don't have to worry about attracting the opposite sex; as long as my financial life is a mess, I don't have to plan for the future. I'm safe. Safe from anyone finding out that I'm just here taking up space. I'm a fraud—I have a good mask in place—strong, confident, charming. If everything I'm hiding behind goes away, what if there's nothing left but ugliness?

As I have helped people work through the challenge of defining and then pursing the vision for the life they want, I have witnessed profound changes in the very fabric of their lives. Not only is the clutter banished and a less-stressed and richer life achieved, but there is also a ripple effect that I don't think anyone foresees. Organizing and decluttering a home becomes the first step in a process that touches every aspect of the person's life. Almost without exception, people reassess their relationships and remove the hurdles that have stunted their emotional lives. Some couples have realized that the life they are living together is more about fear than growth—and have gone their separate ways. Others have realized that major changes were needed if their relationship were to continue. People have lost weight, changed careers, reassessed the way they spent their time, altered the way they interact with their friends and family, and reorganized their priorities. Emotional, social, and spiritual lives have flourished. Removing the clutter from people's lives is so much more than just clearing a desk of unwanted paperwork or getting all that junk out of the garage. Decluttering and organizing is a path to a quality of life that many only dimly glimpse.

The challenge

In this book I will take you far beyond the clutter in your home. Previously I've written extensively about the clutter in our homes and, more recently, about the clutter on our hips. In all my work, however, I see that our homes, our heads, our hearts, and our hips are intimately interconnected. Now we are going to tackle the clutter that fills your head and impedes so many areas of your life. We are going to deal with the underlying feelings that create the clutter that blocks the path to who we want to be—the best version of ourselves.

Now, how did we get from a cluttered closet to jobs, families, relationships, how we communicate, and our sense of well-being? It's really not that much of a stretch. I've seen it again and again in my work. Just like your home, your head is filled with clutter that interferes with how you live your life. Things—physical and emotional—get in the way of finding clarity and achieving your goals. Grocery shopping gets in the way. Bill paying gets in the way. Anger, greed, envy, and a host of other emotions get in the way. All the unfulfilled promises that accompany "the stuff" and that clog the arteries of your home also clog the arteries of your mind and body. Clutter—whether it's in your home or in your mind—causes you to lose motivation, focus, open space, clarity, a place where you can relax and be nurtured. These are the qualities that lead you to a happier, fuller life. When they're lost, so is any chance of achieving what you want in life. Your head is a mess of unreal expectations that get in the way of living your life. The same way you need to actively carve out space in your home, you

5

need to carve a path for yourself in life. You need to make your life happen. This book is a systematic plan for creating a vision of the life you want, identifying and clearing many of the obstacles that stand in your way, and making that vision a reality. You will come to understand more clearly how what you own, how you think, how you interact with others, what you value, and how you approach every aspect of your life can help or impede what should be your most important goal—living the one life you have to the fullest in a way that brings you deep joy and lasting pleasure.

Look to yourself first

Stop for a moment and ponder this: what is it that you want *from* your life? Are there things you want *from* your romantic relationships that you don't get? What do you want *from* your work? Your family? Your finances? Your health? Your spiritual well-being? Are you satisfied in all these areas of your life? If not, what are you doing about it? Actions have consequences, and if you don't act most likely nothing changes. If something is important to you, it should be a priority. So I ask you: What are your priorities? Are they scattered in the clutter of everyday life? Has your life lost its sense of purpose? Do you feel lost, stuck, and confused? If you don't live by your priorities what's important to you is lost and you can't be happy. It's that simple.

Again, think about this: Are you *in* your life? Does the clutter of your life keep you so preoccupied with people, events, failures, or achievements from the past that you are terrified that if you let go of it you will lose a part of yourself? Are you fearful of what tomorrow might bring and so hold on to things "just in case"? Does your stuff take precedence over your relationships, causing friction and arguments? Are you invested in living your most authentic life now or clinging to what you own for dear life?

Dear Peter:
The bottom line is I am living a double life. I am a successful educational consultant. People perceive me as a confident, competent, and intelligent woman. I do very well hiding the shame of my private life. Actually, I'm not doing as well as I used to. I can't find anything when I need it. My credit is a mess. I've gained thirty pounds. I'm exhausted yet can't sleep. I'm single because I can't even think about dating until I get my life together. I think I've shut down. The wear and tear of living this double life is really starting to show. It interferes with my personal and professional life. I tried so many times to conquer my clutter that I no longer trust myself to give it a go. I used to be able to rally and pull it all together last minute for projects or events, but find I can't do it so easily anymore.

I've helped people clear the clutter from the outer spaces—their homes, their rooms, their personal spaces. Now, I'm going to help you take this one step further: We're going to tackle the inner spaces—your head, your emotions, your attitudes. Our task here is to clear the emotional stuff that clutters the six key areas of your life: relationships, work, family, finances, health, and spiritual well-being. If you know my work at all, you know that I don't tolerate the physical clutter that stands between you and the best life you can be living and I won't tolerate the mental clutter, either.

Your home is a reflection of your life. For this reason, I don't believe you can make progress in any area of your life if your home is a mess. But I've written a whole other book about that, so instead of rehashing it here, let's just say that before this book can help you, you must already have a (relatively) clutter-free and organized home. You have to start with a solid foundation, and if your home is not providing you a space of peace and calm, focus and motivation, then it's tough to expect the same in other areas of your life—particularly your head space! First things first—start with your home and then we can move on from there.

What does it take to make changes in your life?

Clarity

Decluttering isn't just simplifying your life. It's having a vision, setting new priorities, and using those notions to get rid of obstacles. If you don't have the life you want, it's not going to fall into your lap. You have to start with the vision of the life you want. That's what I'm going to ask you to do in every area of your life—to begin the process of achieving the life you want by articulating a clear, realistic vision of what that life is.

Self-awareness

I'm just here to give you a not-so-gentle push in the right direction; the only power that will get you there is you. The only path is the one you design. The only obstacles are the ones you buy, create, or imagine. Don't cling to clutter in the form of anger and frustration instead of letting go and changing. All of us know what we should do to achieve our goals, but we often just don't do what needs to be done. Instead, we sit around feeling entitled or overwhelmed, waiting for someone else to make the changes for us. Enough already! Once you have a clear vision for the life you want, you need to take responsibility for achieving that vision. Owning your life, your decisions, and your actions is the first step to initiating real change.

Commitment

Change takes time and is often difficult—it's easier to stay with what we know than to embrace the new and unknown. In our world of instant gratification, we give up too easily, saying, "I tried that and it didn't work." Don't be in a rush to fix every single element of your life in days or weeks. Instead, focus on being honest, fair, and responsible. Clear the clutter from your decision making. Making physical changes to the space where you live takes energy that you can see and quantify, but emotional changes are harder for everyone. However, organization is not something

Dear Peter:

I have been working on decluttering my head for about nine months now. And really, it's much the same as decluttering a room. First, you need to take everything out and sort . . . to see what to keep, what to throw out, and what needs to be given away. I do this mostly through journaling. I pretty much "vomit" (sorry for the term) onto the keyboard and type like crazy, not overthinking, just being totally honest about what's going on in "here." Then I sort.

I keep what it is that I find worthy of my time and effort, I give other people the things/problems that can really only be resolved by them and never really belonged to me in the first place, and the junk that I have held on to for years (okay, my lifetime), I am learning to get rid of.

This is all easier said than done, but so worth the effort. At first, it seemed overwhelming, but now I am embracing the process. The result: I am more content. I am more honest about my needs. My husband of almost twenty-five years says I am easier to live with. Oh, and I have lost seventy pounds.

you do—it's a place where you are and a commitment to living in a particular way. If you're experiencing a nagging feeling of frustration or unease, then it's time to clear the clutter and open your life to what is possible.

So get out your metaphoric garbage bags. Let's clear the path to better decision making, clearer thinking, and a fulfilling, happy life that's as close to your ideal as humanly possible.

Choice and change

Change comes from the choices that you make. By embracing the challenge of decluttering your inner space, you will come to see your life in a new and unclouded way. You will be present, aware, and fully involved in the small and large decisions that will direct your life in new and exciting directions. This process will move you beyond thinking about what you think you might need *for* your home or your life to understanding what you want *from* your life to make it truly and uniquely yours.

If you are struggling with the life you have, if clutter and disorganization are any part of your life—either in your home or in your head or in your heart—then this is a great opportunity to use that experience as a stepping-stone to a richer, more exciting, and more fulfilling place.

Let's get started!

Relationships

You can't make love in a pigsty

Amelia is an attractive, high-powered fashion executive who works long hours and comes home exhausted to her husband, Robert, and an adorable young son. They live in a large, beautiful house in the suburbs of New York City where Amelia loves to garden. To the outside eye, the family seems to have a perfect life, but for more than a year Amelia's job has been a major source of stress. She'd been promised raises and promotions that never seemed to emerge, and Amelia's frustration at work became the main topic of conversation at home. Then Amelia finally got her dream job—and that's when the trouble really started. As soon as her job issues cleared up, Amelia realized she wasn't happy in her marriage. After all those hours she'd spent working in the backyard, trying to make everything perfect, she realized it wasn't. She told Robert he was suffocating her. She just needed space. He looked around their spacious house. It was clean and sparsely furnished. He looked at the clock. It was 9:00 p.m. and she'd just gotten home from work. He barely saw his wife. How could *he* be suffocating her?

I've had countless clients who walk into their cluttered homes and are overwhelmed by a feeling of suffocation. Physical clutter takes its toll on your psyche. Cleaning it up is no easy task, but at least you can see the problem in front of you. And even if you've gone blind to the clutter, the people around you who care about you can still see it. But what happens when the clutter is an invisible barrier that has grown between two people? Relationship clutter is abstract, and clutter that is hard to see is often hard to understand. You can't put it in bags and drop it off at Goodwill—if only it were that easy! So let's talk about what relationship clutter looks like: Does your relationship make you feel anxious instead of calm? Do you feel invaded and overwhelmed or lonely and hopeless? Are you trapped in daily routines that don't work for either of you? Are you deeply unhappy with your partner? Do you have the same arguments without resolution? Have the small problems been left to grow and fester until they've become big problems? How do you find clarity? Are you forgiving or are you entrenched in the belief that your opinion is the better one? How do you set boundaries that work for you and your partner? How do you weather the hard times that inevitably come? And can you admit failure with or without blame and accusation? In this chapter, I'll guide you through the most common forms of relationship clutter and how you can begin to purge them from your life.

Quiz:
Is Your Relationship Cluttered?

1. When you and your partner have a disagreement:
   a. *We fight it out until we understand each other.*
   b. *We wait until we cool down, then find a way to make the peace.*
   c. *We sweep it under the rug—it's the same old argument, why bother?*

2. When you and your partner sit down to a private dinner:
   a. *We're happy to have the time together.*
   b. *It's fine. But let's be honest—most of the time we're watching TV during dinner.*
   c. *It's tense. We never know if we'll end up fighting.*

3. When it comes to your sex life:
   a. *We want and enjoy the same thing.*
   b. *We have different ideas of what and how often, but make compromises.*
   c. *What sex life?*

4. When you and your partner take a vacation:
   a. *We always have a good time—we're glad to have time off together.*
   b. *We have different ideas of how to relax, but we make it work.*
   c. *We go our separate ways—there's just no other option.*

5. When you feel hurt and vulnerable, your partner is:
   a. *The person I turn to for support and unconditional love.*
   b. *A good listener, even if s/he doesn't take my side.*
   c. *Most likely the reason I feel hurt and vulnerable in the first place.*

6. When you have a problem at your job, your partner:
   a. *Listens to me with full and complete attention.*
   b. *Listens at the same time as s/he does something else.*
   c. *May pretend to listen, but doesn't really care.*

7. The relationship you want now and in the future:
   a. *Matches what my partner wants.*
   b. *Isn't exactly what my partner wants, but we're working on compromises.*
   c. *Probably isn't possible with this person, but I can't see a way out.*

8. You and your partner spend your leisure time:
   a. *Together, enjoying the same activities.*
   b. *Sometimes together and sometimes apart, depending on the day.*
   c. *Apart—we have different interests.*

9. When it comes to spending money:
   a. *We see eye-to-eye on what we want and what we can afford.*
   b. *Sometimes we have different priorities, but we know how to survive.*
   c. *We disagree, or even hide expenditures from each other.*

10. Your partner's life view is:
    a. *Similar to mine.*
    b. *Different from mine, but we respect each other.*
    c. *Hard for me to understand.*

Is your relationship cluttered?

If your answers are mostly As:
You and your partner not only communicate well, but you also have the good fortune to share similar interests. Make the most of your compatibility, but don't hold yourselves rigidly to it. If you're in a long-term relationship, your interests might change and diversify over the years. That's okay—you can handle having separate friends and activities. Just make sure you continue to communicate.

If your answers are mostly Bs:
You are not alone. Most people have relationships like yours and there are bumps along the road. Sometimes you see them coming and sometimes you don't. Regardless, you try to hold on tight and work to get past them. The key to seeing clearly is to let your priorities guide you. If the relationship is a priority, then winning each argument or having a perfect date every night you spend together becomes less important. Finding the best balance for the two of you comes first. Focus on that and you'll find that your issues are minimized in importance without either one of you sacrificing your sense of self.

If your answers are mostly Cs:
This is a tough relationship for you. Whether it's a new relationship where you haven't learned to communicate, or a seasoned relationship where you've all but given up, now is the time to learn (or relearn) how to communicate. Look at the differences you have with your partner. How much conflict can you endure? What toll is it taking on you? Relationships take work, and yours needs it. Clear the clutter that's tripping you up now, before it's too late.

Imagine the relationship you want

Whether you are in a relationship already or looking to start one, the path to change always begins with a vision. Whenever I meet a new client, whether they are looking to clear the clutter, lose weight, or improve a relationship, I always have them answer the same question:

What is the life I want to live?

If you've heard me talk or read any of my books, you've undoubtedly heard me ask this question many times, and with good reason. I know no better way to launch the forces of change than to wrestle honestly with this question. We all have different internal notions of the life we wish were ours. But it takes work to stay focused on that life. I see clutter build up in homes slowly, over the years, until without realizing it the people who live there lose access to garages, whole closets, then entire rooms, and sometimes even sections of the house. Little by little, they lose their dream

Dear Peter:

After listening to your audio book *Does This Clutter Make My Butt Look Fat?*, I realized that most of my depression and my very many separations were due to clutter. My husband is a pack rat. In the times we separated, my home with three kids was clean and very peaceful. When we would get back together the chaos and mess would begin again, then would come the depression, poor eating, and once again another separation. He began dealing with his clutter on the last separation (number seven). He moved back and so did the major clutter. He has been listening to your book this time, and we have removed eight large garbage bags of clutter. It has brought hope back into our relationship, and we are doing things as a family. We are daily working at least one hour a day at removing the clutter.

I believe that the clutter in his life has held him back from working, has greatly affected his health, dreams, and hopes. As the clutter is removed, he has stopped sleeping as much. Thank you for taking the time to write. It has truly been life changing.

So clutter can and will destroy lives. If I ever remarry or when my kids do, I will have them look at the place their potential spouse lives in. It is at the top of the list now.

homes and, along with them, their dreams. The clutter has cut them off from what they really want from their lives.

In this same way, the clutter of every day can build up around your vision of the ideal relationship until you have trouble seeing it. Think about how your relationships figure into the question of what you want from your life. (In this chapter I talk primarily about love relationships, but the process here can be applied to any important relationships in your life.) In your ideal relationship, how do you and your partner spend time? How do you feel when you're together? What are your mornings like? How do you divide up responsibilities? How involved are you in each other's work and social lives? Do you share friends and interests? Do you have or will you build a family together? How deep and long-term is your commitment or would you like it to be? What qualities and range of emotion do you expect from your relationship? Do you *like* each other? Are you a silly and outgoing couple or a serious, hard-working couple?

Finding a vision for a relationship is different from finding a vision for your home, or your work, or your body because there is one other person involved, and that person is a unique individual, with a complex set of emotions, habits, and desires that match up to your ideal in imperfect, inconsistent, and unpredictable ways. At the core of a successful relationship is a shared vision. But unless you're incredibly lucky, that vision doesn't emerge fully formed the day you meet your partner. No, relationships are about growth and change, compromise, consideration, and balance.

Think about that. A shared vision. Shared goals. Compromise, consideration, and balance. These qualities aren't anywhere on paper, much less written on your sleeve when you see a stranger across a crowded room. Even if you hired an old-fashioned matchmaker, it would be impossible to identify and match the infinite ingredients that add up to compatibility. You need to work, explore, and experiment with each other.

Even after you've found happiness together, it doesn't come with a lifetime guarantee. Over time, the clutter of every day can obscure your priorities and cloud your vision.

Before you clear the clutter of your relationship, let's define your vision.

What do you want from your relationship?

A million ideas and images may flow into your head, but let me help you get started.

• Companionship
What sort of company do you expect from your mate? Does he offer you support or comfort in your time of need? Is she your best friend? Does he help you make decisions? Is she the person with whom you take pleasure in your successes?

• Life partner/family
How long have you been together? How long do you think you'll be together? Do you see the two of you getting old together and, if so, how will your life change as you age?

Do you want to have a family together? Do you share the same views of what that family life is like? What role does each of you play? What hopes do you have for your family?

Are you happy? What would you change about this relationship if you could (in yourself and your behavior as well as your partner and his or hers)? What sacrifices will you have to make or are you willing to make to create this life together? Is this what you thought your life would be like with this partner when you got married? If you were totally honest with yourself—would you stay?

• Fun
Do you and your partner have the same definition of fun? Do you have shared interests and friends or do you lead separate lives?

When it comes to free time, does one of you like to stay out late and the other prefer quiet time at home? What counts for fun in your daily lives together? Can you have a good time together doing everyday activities like grocery shopping or cooking dinner, or do you need to set aside special time to create relaxed or romantic moments when you can really unwind? Does one partner shoulder more of the responsibility for the upkeep in the relationship: kids, bills, household chores, remembering and making outside commitments?

- **Love and be loved**

Is your relationship grounded by a constant, reliable love? Do you feel confident that when you meet up with your partner at the end of a hard day, you'll find a warm, comforting reception? Does the very existence of your partner give you a sense of security, purpose, and well-being?

- **Sexual fulfillment**

How important is sex in your relationship? Do you and your partner view the importance of sex in your relationship in the same way? Does one of you want more or less? Have your sexual needs changed over time? Are they still in sync with your partner's? Can you speak openly about your desires, fantasies, or complaints?

Clear the clutter of unreal expectations

The relationship scale is a conversation starting point. I want you and your partner to take the time to really discuss your answers and share your vision with each other for your ideal relationship. Sometimes the longer you are with a person, the more you take them for granted. Often you come to expect your partner to know what you want without ever explaining it. We assume—

Activity
What's Important in a Relationship?

Examine the starter list of relationship traits below. Together with your partner, brainstorm others that are important to you both and add them to the list. Then, separately, you and your partner rate the relationship traits on a scale of one (most important) to five (least important). Then share your results. Examine those traits where your scores were significantly different—are you surprised? Even if the answers don't surprise you, they will definitely get you talking.

THE RELATIONSHIP SCALE

Trait	Me	My Partner
Honesty		
Sexual attraction/ fulfillment		
Fidelity		
Humor		
Emotional support		
Common interests		

Activity
Define Your Vision for Your Relationship

As a way of clarifying your thoughts, complete the following table. If you're in a relationship, ask your partner to do the same and compare your responses. If you're single, use this activity to think through your expectations for what you want in a relationship.

Words that describe the relationship you currently have:

- _____

- _____

- _____

- _____

- _____

- _____

Words that describe the relationship you want to have:

- _____

- _____

- _____

- _____

- _____

- _____

Describe what your ideal relationship would be like:

What do you have to change to allow that ideal relationship to emerge?

not necessarily in a bad way—that our partners are in sync with our own thoughts. But remember—no one is a mind reader! Admit it, sometimes you don't even know what your own true expectations might be, so how can you expect your partner to know for you? If you do expect a mind reader, no wonder your partner keeps failing you. Remember that along with expectations come responsibilities. You can't ask your partner for clarity and support without being willing to give clarity and support in return. Nonetheless, relationships aren't an eye-for-an-eye exchange. Everyone has unique and important needs. You must be willing to address your partner's needs—even when they're different from yours—to make this process work. Both of you should let go of unrealistic expectations and work together to define a practical vision for your relationship.

Watch out for obstacles

Even if you're not having big problems in your relationship, over time the same bad habits tend to accumulate and stick around—just like the paperwork in your home office or the extra clothes in your closet—causing trouble between even the best-matched couples. Before you begin to clean up your relationship, let's identify some obstacles to avoid as you clear the path to a clutter-free relationship.

Cluttered priorities

Life is busy. You're juggling work, family, relationships—all the major life categories that this book deals with. It's easy to forget what's most important when you're focused on just getting through another day with no major disasters. When you lose track of priorities, all sorts of problems crop up.

Lost boundaries

When your priorities are cluttered, you lose track of your own needs. Taking care of yourself means establishing boundaries—especially boundaries that define how much of yourself you devote to others. If you're stuck in a pattern of overhandling someone else's life or handing over your life to someone else—hanging out with *his* friends, doing *her* laundry, supporting *his* interests—your resentment will build over time. And what is that resentment? New clutter on top of existing clutter.

Selfishness

The flip side of not setting appropriate personal boundaries is selfishness. Your wife plans a Saturday tennis match without consulting you, so you're stuck home all afternoon, waiting for the plumber. Or you give your best friend, who rubs your husband the wrong way, keys to the house. When you lose track of how much you value your relationship, you put a higher priority on your own needs and interests. Most relationships have trouble weathering this imbalance. No matter how busy you are and how hard it is to find a balance, you have to always remember to value your partner's needs as much as you do your own.

Withdrawal

We withdraw from problems when overcoming them seems like too much work, or is too scary, or requires admitting truths we don't want to face. Instead of working on what you have, it can seem easier to switch to autopilot and coast through the relationship. Most of us can go through the motions of being a girlfriend/boyfriend/wife/husband in our sleep. All it takes is showing up at dinner, talking about your day, crawling into bed, and throwing a token arm around your partner. Running on autopilot means you don't really listen to your partner, or don't really care. Autopilot means that you settle for less than you can be and live your relationship by habit.

Autopilot never delivers the easy cruise it promises. The straight path of love and understanding falters when it is left unattended. As soon as you hit unexpected turbulence, autopilot goes haywire. If you don't face your problems head-on, you're not living in the present. You either cling to the past, when things were rosier, or you look to the future and change partners instead of working on a relationship. I've seen people fill up their basements with clutter and then rent storage spaces because they "have no room." They have plenty of room, they're just unwilling to do the work to make it useable. The same is true for people who look for happiness outside a committed relationship before working to fix what they already have.

Many people find that as the newness of a relationship wears off, the same unresolved problems come along to clutter it up, and rather than deal with those issues they choose to leave the relationship. But the next great thing is rarely the answer. If you don't deal with the issues, you carry them from relationship to relationship and there they sit between you and your partner: a big bag of unexamined clutter.

You may believe there's one perfect person out there for you and that if you can just find him everything will be perfect, but I can tell you that even the most compatible couple has to work hard to sustain a long-term relationship and to create those perfect moments that add up to a happy partnership.

Cluttered emotions

When love is at stake, multiple emotions come into play. All the baggage you like to blame on your parents gets piled up alongside all the baggage your partner throws on the pile. Cluttered emo-

tions prevent you from acting on your true feelings. The words you choose, the small everyday interactions that should be pleasant and aren't, the fights you get into, none of these is governed by the love you feel for your partner and the hopes and dreams you have for the relationship. Instead, you are subjecting your partner to the emotional clutter that came with you into the relationship and needs to be cleared out.

Anger

I'm no physicist, but I can tell you that anger, like clutter that fills a space, is conserved. The clutter didn't appear overnight and it won't disappear overnight. You have to get rid of it box by box, garbage bag by garbage bag, issue by issue. Similarly, anger doesn't appear out of nowhere and it doesn't disappear into thin air. All that energy has to go someplace. This is why old anger can come back to haunt you or your partner. And this is why if you never deal with the anger that you brought to the relationship, or the anger that grows out of unresolved issues, it will rear its ugly head over and over again in unexpected ways that you can't imagine. How can you get rid of anger that's been around so long it seems like either an impossible habit to break or an irreversible part of you or your partner's personality? Well, that anger is clutter, and you need to face it, deal with it, dismantle it, and throw it away, piece by piece.

Passive-aggressive behavior

Passive-aggressive behavior is a form of anger, but it's anger in disguise. Some of us get very good at hiding our anger, but, as I said, that doesn't make the anger disappear. Instead, it can take the form of being passive-aggressive. The wife who keeps "forgetting" to hang up her towel. The boyfriend who "teases" you about your outfit in front of your colleagues. A person clever enough to

use passive aggression will most likely, when accused of using it, deny, deny, deny. We are complex beings, but I'm going to help you make every effort to identify and get rid of the passive aggression that stands in the way of a healthy, happy relationship.

Fear

Fear is a sneaky emotion. You don't have to be quaking in your shoes, breaking a sweat, heart pounding, to be living in fear. Fear comes to play in relationships in two forms: fear of moving forward and fear of getting out. Think about moving forward. There's a whole lot to be afraid of. Is this the right person? How can you know? What if you change your mind? What if s/he does? How do you know you can love one person for the rest of your life— you've never done *that* before, and if you don't get it right the first time, you'll be a *failure*. On the other hand, even if your relationship is no good, it can be very hard to leave. Loneliness looms. It can seem better to be unsatisfied in a relationship than to be miserable and alone. Fear is why we hold on to objects that we don't use. What you know—be it your flawed relationship or the false comfort of unused possessions—is easier and more comfortable than what you don't know. So when you're caught in this kind of situation, you tend to go with the easy rather than with the good. But is that your goal? To stay in an unsatisfying relationship for fear of being alone? The answer is in your heart, and you're going to find it.

Low self-esteem

Fear and low self-esteem are cousins. Both paralyze you because you expect change to worsen your circumstances instead of bettering them. And your circumstances are probably not that great to begin with. If you don't honor, respect, and love yourself, then why should someone else? If you don't value yourself, you are all

the more likely to stay with someone who doesn't value you. Low self-esteem means bad choices. You choose bad mates. You stay with them even when they treat you badly. You don't stand up for yourself. Your expectations for yourself are low and your choices reflect that.

Cluttered communication

When does a disagreement turn into a fight? Is it when your voices get loud? Is it when the disagreement escalates, so instead of figuring out who is responsible for doing last night's dishes you're now arguing about the tone of voice someone used? Or is it when the disagreement changes paths entirely? The issue of the dishes explodes and now everything is fair game—from forgetting birthdays to spending too much money to who is putting more energy into the relationship. Disagreements are inevitable in any relationship. The challenge is to disagree productively, so that you stay on the subject, don't escalate, and come to a resolution.

The key to productive disagreements is clearing the clutter from your communication—and not just when you're fighting.

Grievances

When you're trying to clean out your basement, you can't just buy storage bins and move everything around. Relocating stuff doesn't clear the clutter—you have to get rid of it. The same principle is true for communication. Without good communication, grievances are never completely laid to rest. Instead, they accumulate over time. Then every time you fight you end up dragging up stuff from the past. The same issues come back again and again, compounded by how they were dealt with (or not) in the last fight. It's a downhill spiral from there. Communication is the key to ending grievances once and for all.

Win/lose arguments

Some of us just don't like to lose. Losing an argument means more than admitting that you were wrong. It means losing power and losing control. How can you change your goal from winning the argument to ending the argument? If it's hard for you to let go of an argument, you need to train yourself to step back and look at the situation in front of you. How much do you care about what you're fighting for? Apologizing and admitting defeat may seem hard, but what's even more strenuous is continuing to argue. Is the goal to be right? Is the goal to get your way? Or is the goal to find a peaceful, reasonable resolution and move on with your day? As we proceed, you're going to work on keeping your goals in mind even in the heat of the moment.

Overtalking

This seems like a no-brainer. If you talk over someone, you effectively cut them off and can't hear what they're saying, thereby turning a conversation into a monologue. Now, I want you to think about this behavior because we all do it sometimes. You know when your partner is talking and you've already figured out what you're going to say next? Even though it's in your head, *that's* overtalking, too. Your mind is not focused on what your partner is trying to communicate. Instead, you're focused on making your point. You're not really "in" the discussion. That may work on high school debate teams, but it's no way to foster true understanding or healthy communication.

Cluttered priorities. Cluttered emotions. Cluttered communication. These are the obstacles that interfere with your vision of the ideal relationship.

Activity
What's Getting in the Way of My Ideal Relationship?

Reviewing the sections above, write down the obstacles that stand in the way of the relationship you want.

- _____

- _____

- _____

Declutter your relationship

Unfortunately, it's not as easy as putting the messy parts of your relationship in garbage bags and carting them away. Just as with physical clutter, decluttering the obstacles to a healthy relationship is a process that first requires changing the way you think. That change starts with the clear vision that you and your partner develop together. Change will come day by day, in every decision you make. Here's how to work on achieving that vision.

Commit time

I'm not asking you to sign up for a weekend workshop or to commit to couples' therapy once a week until the end of time (although that can be very helpful). But I need you to acknowledge that changes take time. If what you want is a long-term relationship, then you need to commit to long-term work, not because you have to but because you want to. You'll always be working on your relationship to some extent—and that's a great thing. You may have periods of slacking off, or overwhelming times when your partner has to cover for you, but the point is that you need to commit for the long haul. You need to be firmly "in" the relationship—heart, soul, mind, and body. All of you! Commit, and commit together. This is not "his issue" or "her problem." Don't put it all on the other person. Your relationship has settled where it is for a reason. You're both responsible and until you get to "our answer," there can be no resolution.

Time to connect

Common ground. Just as clutter accumulates over time, age shows in a relationship. You may have met your husband parasailing on a tropical island, but ten years and three kids later parasailing seems irresponsible and that tropical island is a ten-hour plane ride out of reach. When I work with people to declutter their homes, we spend time with each object, facing the truth of whether it really belongs in their home and in their lives. What's with the dusty skates? Did they once love to ice-skate? Will they ever again? Are they holding on to high school football mementos because they represent an unfulfilled dream? I want you to contemplate the interests and activities that attracted you to each other and how they have changed. Do you still have those interests? Do you still participate in those activities? Do you want to or have you developed other interests that you'd like to share with your partner?

Try to spend time together in the places and ways that you both enjoy. This doesn't mean you should pull out your miniskirt and dancing shoes and pull an all-nighter at the local hot spot. But would it kill you to make out in your car? You may not have time for the romantic dates that filled your courting days, but look for ways to recapture that feeling. If you can't go out to dinner and a movie every week, commit to doing it once a month. If you're too old for dance clubs, sign up for a salsa class. Lazing in front of the TV may be relaxing, but you can laze in front of the TV with your mother. It doesn't make for a very sexy relationship. Every fire needs a little fuel—what's yours?

Date night. Corny? Maybe. But if you have to schedule time to make it happen, then you need to schedule time to make it happen! Even if you don't have kids you should still schedule a date night. What's most critical about planning a date night is the time you're committing to your relationship. Date night is more than making a commitment to spending time together. It's you and your partner both declaring that you're willing to invest in the relationship. Trust me, it's worth the effort.

Time to grow

Everybody changes over time, so every relationship has to make room for change. Some changes are exciting (your partner finally joins a gym and develops the body you've both always wanted him to have) and some are tough to weather (your partner loses her job and with it her sense of purpose). It's easy for me to tell you that you need to be supportive and open to change. But I don't think there's anyone for whom it comes naturally to say, "You've been wearing the same loafers for twenty years and now you want lime green cowboy boots? Fabulous!" Change is scary, even threatening. Because if your partner changes his taste in cowboy boots today, he might change his taste in lovers tomorrow. But resisting change will only create distance in a relationship. You don't have to be onboard and gung ho with every new development, but remember to respect your partner's evolving thoughts, dreams, tastes, and opinions. Even the most understanding among us has to take a deep breath and remember what's important before saying, "It's okay that you lost your job." Or, "I'll talk about moving across the country if that's what you want." Or "Great boots!" That's what I want you to work on—keeping that relationship vision in your mind so that you slow down enough to respond to your partner not as an extension of you, but as a separate, interesting, worthwhile person.

The same thing goes when it comes to your own desires. I want you to allow yourself change. If those boots are attractive to you, try them on! If you never liked cooking, say so! I'm not saying it's okay to be selfish—you're still in a partnership—but look for ways to experiment with your ideas and desires without stirring up conflict. Try exploring the excitement of change or the new together—you might be surprised. Finding that balance should be part of the fabric of your relationship.

Communicate

In every relationship there are disagreements. Some disagreements end relationships. If you're in a long-term relationship, you've figured out a way to survive your disagreements. That's why you're still together. You've come up with ways to forge a peace. Maybe you say, "I'm sorry" and expect that to be the end. Maybe you give in. Maybe you don't speak for hours, even days, then forgive each other without further discussion. But just because the argument is over doesn't mean all is well. If you don't work through your differences, they accumulate. That's right: Your grievances accumulate like unpaid bills or those long-unopened boxes in the garage, haunting your household, cluttering your home, and serving as a constant reminder that you aren't living the life you wish you had.

Learn to listen

This may sound ridiculously basic, but the first step toward averting and recovering from arguments is to listen well at all times, and I want you to start practicing now. Most of us are simply not good listeners—we have so much invested in what we have to say that we miss much of what the other person is saying or we are preoccupied and only give half our attention to the conversation. Good listening can't happen if you are watching TV, checking e-mail on your cellphone, playing a video game, leafing through a magazine, or doing any of the other ten thousand distracting things there are in the world. We can all stand to improve our listening, but if you included laziness, selfishness, or overtalking on

Listening well means:

Eye contact. Be the good student you never were. Look directly at your partner the way a teacher would want a child to pay attention in class. If you try this a couple of times, you will realize that going through the motions of paying attention forces you to actually do it.

Hands-free. This means absolutely no cellphone in hand while you're talking to your partner. If you're sitting at a computer, put your hands in your lap and turn to face your partner. Put down the newspaper. Turn the TV off. No multitasking!

One-sided discussions. Give your partner space. Every other time he or she makes a complaint or brings up an issue, instead of countering with your side of the story or your own issue, try focusing exclusively on your partner. This is not a business negotiation. Address her issue without bartering with your own needs.

your list of the obstacles that stand in the way of your ideal relationship, you need to pay particular attention now.

Beginning, middle, and end

No matter how well you listen, fights are bound to happen. Every disagreement should have a beginning, a middle, and an end. This is the route to diffusing long-term grievances. One of my clients, Elizabeth, describes a small fight she had with her husband, Charlie. It was a fall day and they were setting out on a walk with their two young children. Seeing the Sunday newspaper on the lawn reminded Elizabeth that they had to stop delivery for their upcoming vacation. When she mentioned this to Charlie, he said, "Oh, we've got plenty of time." She responded, "No, we don't. You have to tell them pretty far in advance, which you would know if you'd ever been the one to stop the paper." Ouch. Charlie wasn't going to take that kind of abuse. "Sorry I'm such a disappointment to you," he said in a voice dripping with sarcasm. She apologized, but the damage was done. They walked in silence until Charlie cooled down, and that was the end of it.

But it wasn't the end of it. Because nothing was resolved. Instead, the issue that had sparked the incident was stuffed away, just like those clothes in your closet from two years ago that still have the tags attached! And if you know me, you know how I feel about never-worn clothes and overstuffed closets. Arguments, like closets, don't resolve themselves—unaddressed, the problem only festers and gets worse. Look at your junk mail if you're not sure what I mean!

I've met Charlie. He seems like a very nice guy. So my question to Elizabeth was, "What's this about? What does the newspaper represent?" She thought for a while. Finally she said, "I run the household and work part-time. I have no problem with that arrangement. But I don't think Charlie has any idea how much time I spend doing stupid things like paying bills and getting repairs done." We left it at that, but three days later Elizabeth called me to say, "I couldn't stop thinking about the newspaper thing. I was wrong about the problem. There are just too many small chores. It's annoying, I'm tired of it, and I take it out on Charlie. I don't blame him for getting angry. I can't imagine him ever speaking that way to me."

Sure, the reason Elizabeth lashed out matters. But think about how hard it was for her to understand and explain why she did it. If she doesn't understand herself, if it takes her this long to examine and articulate the meaning behind a throw-away comment she made on the front lawn, how is Charlie supposed to understand her without her help and guidance? Most of us make offhanded comments that turn into arguments. Yes, it's ideal to put your brain in gear before you engage your mouth, but all of us talk before we think more often than we'd like to admit. The only way to make sure your arguments truly end is to see them through. This is how adults resolve conflict in a healthy and productive way—try it, you'll be surprised at just how good it feels.

Take responsibility and clean up the mess you've made. How? Be honest with yourself. Learn to unravel the meaning behind the choices you make in your relationship that lead to conflict. You can do it together in a cooler moment, or do what Elizabeth did— figure it out for yourself and explain to your partner later in a calm and honest way. Maybe Elizabeth will be able to stop herself from lashing out next time. But even if she doesn't, at least she has been open and honest with herself and Charlie about what she did and is working hard to move past the behavior so she doesn't keep repeating it. Maybe Charlie will be able to take her next outbreak in stride because they've spoken about it and he has more insight into Elizabeth's behavior and is helping her work on it

Get to the heart of the issue

It probably goes without saying that the middle of the fight is where emotional clutter gets in the way. In the heat of the moment, anger, defensiveness, and myriad other emotions interfere with your ability to see clearly and act based on your priorities. Everyone knows that when you see red the best thing to do is to stop and take a deep breath. But knowing and doing are very different. You know you shouldn't buy another pair of shoes or eat another cookie, but you do. What if you actually stopped long enough to inhale deeply and exhale completely? Would it change the argument? There's only one way to find out. And in the mid-fight moment that you create, I want you to summon your priorities. How important is this fight to you? Can the discussion be had in a calm, loving manner? Can you elevate the fight from accusation and blame to explanation and understanding? If you can, you'll be doing good work that will benefit your relationship in the long run.

End fights peacefully

Are you too focused on winning arguments? If that is one of your obstacles, you need to work on having better fights. That's right, as strange as it sounds, I want you to learn how to have a healthy fight. Fear of anger or conflict, an imbalanced desire to win every argument, control issues, passive-aggressive behavior, all of these are clutter that interfere with your ability to argue with clarity and direction. Stick with the issue. Don't make it personal. Don't hit below the belt. Accept that the person you are arguing with is not the enemy, merely someone who happens to disagree with you at the moment. It's not a life-and-death conflict!

If your arguments have bad habits—they always end in tears or with one partner storming out of the room—try, in a peaceful moment, to talk about what you both can do to break the pattern.

Activity
Disagreement Worksheet

Preferably with your partner, use the questions below to identify the clutter that gets in the way of productive arguments.

1. Do you keep your fights focused on a single issue?
2. Does one of you feel accused and/or get defensive? Why?
3. Do you have incompatible styles of arguing or come from families where fighting was very different? How can you reconcile these differences?
4. Do you both put aside your anger to listen?
5. Does one of you always have to win?
6. At the end of a disagreement, do you need time to cool down? How much time?
7. After a fight, does your anger go away or does it get carried over into the next fight?
8. Name one thing your partner could work on to improve the productivity of your fights.
9. Name one thing you could work on to improve the productivity of your fights.

Assume that you *will* fight. It's inevitable, and it's healthy. Now, how can you do it productively?

Establish and respect the basic premise
Ideally, relationships are partnerships, but have you ever stopped to consider who is truly on your team? Who is on your side as your teammate, cheerleader, supporter, and backup? It's a great

question to consider. If your first response in answering this question is not your partner, then there's a serious problem. The best way to deal with tough relationship discussions is to start from the point of who is on your team and what is the basic premise that keeps you together.

While incredibly simple, I have found this concept of "the basic premise" to be one of the most powerful forces in relationships. As partners, your basic premise might well be "I love you, I want to be with you. You are the most important person in the world to me. If any of this changes, I promise I will tell you." If you have this premise firmly in your mind, and keep reminding yourself of it, then every conversation between you and your partner has a foundation of love, respect, and mutual support. Having a basic premise is not just about words—it's about a basis of communicating and a way of being with each other that nourishes a clear relationship and helps keep clutter at bay. In this context, if your partner says "that dress doesn't look good on you," what he means is that the dress doesn't look good on you— not that he doesn't love you or is trying to belittle you. Or if your wife says, "That man is incredibly handsome," it doesn't mean that she loves you any less. The basic principle of open, honest, nonjudgmental communication should be an anchor that holds steady what's important in your relationship.

The basic premise provides a filter through which you can view all interactions with your partner. It gives you security and faith in the genuineness of what you are sharing with each other. It becomes a touchstone against which every exchange and interaction can be measured. With a shared understanding, each partner knows that the end goal is what is best for both of you. It's about building the relationship and arriving at a place that works for you equally. If you haven't spoken with your partner about the basic premise of your relationship, try it. You'll be surprised at how it clears the way for more direct, honest, and productive communication.

Be the person you'd want to come home to
Think about what it's like to come home to a messy home. You open the door and any positive feeling dissolves. You enter and are greeted by a feeling of suffocation. I've said it a million times—you can take control of that clutter one step at a time.

A cluttered home makes you feel overwhelmed, anxious, and stressed-out. Now think about what it is like to come home to you. Does your partner open the door to a warm, welcoming environment or to a feeling of dread? Would you want to hear your first words of the day and your last words of the night? The clutter that accumulates in your home isn't just the old newspapers or magazines, the kids' toys or the craft supplies in the spare bedroom. The way you talk, your reactions, your off-the-cuff remarks, even your body language—this is the "clutter" I am talking about. All of this is clutter as real and overwhelming as that stuff piled untouched on the dining room table.

The last thing I'm recommending is that you put on a Stepford wife or husband smile and pretend everything is perfect. But in order to succeed in fulfilling your vision, you have to participate. You have to communicate. You have to be "in" the relationship. You have to make it exist. Your partner isn't the enemy. If he or she is, well, that's a problem for another book, but one you have to deal with now. Be nice to each other, even if it takes more effort than you want to give, because if one partner lives in fear of the other's bad mood, communication suffers and trust slowly erodes. Even as you work through some of the toughest moments in your relationship, both of you should start by promising to keep a core of stability. Commit to a minimum level of civility You owe it to each other.

The roommate standard

Don't treat your lover worse than you would treat a roommate. Would you storm into a roommate's room and interrupt whatever she was doing to say, "I can't believe you left your dishes in the sink again!" No, you'd wait for a good moment and say, "We need to talk about the dishes . . ." Doesn't the person you love deserve at least the same level of respect you gave your college roommate?

Checking in

Where clutter (physical and emotional) is a problem in a home, one technique I strongly recommend is for couples to ask each other every night before they fall asleep, "What could I have done differently for you today?" This question is a great way to check in with each other and clearly expresses your openness to change. It reminds your partner that you care about his or her daily experience. It invites discussion without argument. It brings small conflicts to the surface so they don't have the opportunity to grow and fester. It ensures that relationship clutter doesn't have an opportunity to accumulate and take over. Better to do the dishes after every meal rather than let them accumulate for a week, agreed?

No pop quizzes

Don't test your partner by setting up situations where he will fail. Because guess what? He *will* fail. And where does that get you? Don't passively hope for a Valentine's Day surprise and then get angry when it doesn't appear. If you know your partner isn't good at gift giving, why make that the criterion by which you judge him? Lead by example; instead of focusing on what's missing, plan something you'll both enjoy. Make it fun and your partner will see why it's worth investing the time and effort.

42

Clean up your language

One easy tip I can give you for clearing the clutter of poor communication is to make sure you're using a "way I'd like to be spoken to" voice. Yes, go back to grade school and remember everything Mrs. ——— (fill in the name of your third-grade teacher) told you about using your best "inside voice." No sarcasm. No yelling. No muttered dismissals. First, listening to yourself will slow you down enough to take a deep breath before you unthinkingly attack your partner. And secondly, "the way I'd like to be spoken to" voice is more likely to be heard and understood by your partner. But even when your partner's voice grates on you, try to listen to what he's really saying. This should go without saying, but don't ever call your partner a nag. "Stop nagging" is a nasty way of saying, "Stop reminding me to do something that you want me to do but aren't sure I'll get done." Nagging is a two-way street. The naggee has the power to stop the nagger. Let's break down the nag. Are you actually planning to follow through on the task? When? If you're stalling, get to the bottom of why. So you hate writing thank-you notes. Do you plan to do it eventually? If you commit to a time and let your partner know when the chore is complete, you'll put an end to the nagging.

When I deal with clutter issues in blended families, or with couples who have come together later in life, one hurdle I always encounter has to do with language. The moment I hear, "This is my chair" or "That's her desk," I can pinpoint a fundamental problem—it's the "his, hers, but not ours" phenomenon. Until couples see their life together as a commitment to each other and can talk in terms of "ours," there's little chance for progress. To address this, I have often recommended that newly together couples sell items that they brought into the relationship—especially pieces that are causing friction—and use the combined money to

Activity
Practice Communicating

Fill out the chart below. Ask your partner to answer the same questions separately and then compare your answers. Your responses will guide how you both work to declutter your relationship.

What I love about you:

What I think you love about me:

What I am afraid of:

What I need from you:

What I think you need from me:

find pieces that they both love. This can be a model to follow for so many areas of a relationship.

If you're in search of a partner
Just as it gets in the way in a relationship, the clutter of all your past hopes and disappointments can get in the way when you are searching for a mate. You need to make sure you approach this quest realistically, with an open mind, and by open mind I mean a clear, clutter-free mind. When you think about what you want in a partner, don't rattle off a list of Seinfeldian turnoffs. Get to the core of your needs and remember that it's tough to get what you can't give. When you meet potential partners, keeping those core needs clear and at the forefront will help guide you to the right partner.

Set boundaries

When I clear the clutter in people's houses, I don't pretend to be a magician. The solution to clutter is very simple: You only have the space you have and you need to work within the limits of your physical space. You can't have so many kitchen appliances and gizmos that there's no counter space left to prepare food. You can only have as many pairs of jeans as will hang reasonably in your closet. The same logic applies to relationships—honor and respect your space, honor and respect your partner and friends. You need to set limits that make sense for the life you're living and preserve the sacredness of the relationship.

Are you checking your e-mails during a romantic dinner? Do you bring your work to bed with you? No matter who you are or what your relationship is like, the first step toward setting boundaries is to stop multitasking. Be where you are and be when you are. Draw lines between work and home, and make sure that

Activity
Declutter and Balance Your Expectations

Create a mental image of the partner you are looking for. Consider what's worked and what hasn't in past relationships. When you have some clear thoughts, complete the following table.

What I need in a partner:

What I offer a partner:

What I like but don't require in a relationship:

What I learned from past relationships and don't want to repeat:

What I should work on in future relationships:

these lines represent your priorities, preserve yourself, and re-spect your partner.

One of the toughest hurdles to overcome in a relationship is selfishness. Looking out for your own interests is natural. It's wise. Everyone does it. But at some point, self-protection inevita-bly crosses over into selfishness. Do you act as though your free time is more precious than your partner's? Do you demand more than you are willing to give? Or do you feel like your partner is oblivious to your needs and desires?

I know one couple who tried to solve their conflicts surround-ing household chores by creating a chart which tracked, minute by minute, how much time each one spent doing housework. The chart included everything from the minutes it took to put the kitchen garbage down the chute in the hallway to the hour it took to vacuum their apartment. At the end of the week they calculated their totals. The person who had done less work (in this case, it was always the husband) had to spend the time he owed his wife by giving her a back massage. I appreciated the elaborate efforts they were making to achieve equity, but ultimately this method didn't work. Why? Because now the wife had evidence—on paper—showing how little her husband did around the house. She didn't like doing housework any more than he and the mas-sage didn't soothe her anger at what she saw as his selfishness.

So how to combat selfishness? Choose your battles. Isolate the moments when it feels like your spouse isn't thinking of you. Choose one activity or behavior that you'd like him or her to mod-ify. When you bring it to the table, make it part of a larger conver-sation where you ask if there's any area where your partner feels like you could pay more attention to his needs.

The flip side of selfishness is selflessness. Being the martyr in a relationship can make everyone happy for a while. The martyr gets to feel generous and superior. The martyr's partner gets treated like a king or a queen, having all of his or her needs prioritized. But the martyr/king dynamic not only inflates the king's ego, it also takes its toll on the martyr. Martyrs tend to be pressure cookers, and when they burst it isn't pretty. As with everything in life, it's important to always work to find a balance. Be giving, but

Activity
Make Concrete Rules to
Preserve Your Relationship

Using the examples below for inspiration, both you and your partner should write down the rules you think necessary to protect your boundaries.

I need a half day of alone time at some point during the weekend.

I promise not to interrupt you when you're reading the paper.

I won't take work calls after 7:00 p.m.

We have to find a way to keep the dogs from sleeping in the bed with us.

don't give all of yourself or you'll wake up one day and realize you have no idea who you are.

Make changes

You can't fix a relationship alone. Both parties need to agree to change, but neither of you should sacrifice who you are to make that change. The only way to make changes that work for both of you is to verbalize what's important to each of you and to both of you, and then make choices based on your shared vision. Together, decide what behaviors are the biggest threats to your shared goals and figure out solutions that work for both of you.

Activity
Define Threats and Propose Modifications

Together with your partner, come up with solutions for behaviors you both agree need to change:

Current behavior	Modification
Comes home and grouses at the kids.	Takes fifteen minutes alone to unwind.

Baggage

When I clean up homes, I always say, "It's not about the stuff." What this means is that there is never clutter without an underlying reason for it. The reasons for physical clutter vary from fear to anger, from passive-aggression to low self-esteem, from the need for control or comfort to dealing with trauma or some form of loss. Tapping into that reason is the first step toward clearing the clutter. The same is true for emotional clutter. For some people, just opening the doors of communication works miracles. You may find that clearing the air with your partner on a regular basis breathes new life into your relationship.

Don't expect miracles

The first thing I asked you to do was to commit time to this process. You may be working to clear out years of clutter in your relationship. The clutter of the past from long before this relationship started may be getting in your way. Clearing out the clutter and breaking these patterns take time, communication, honesty, self-reflection, practice, and hard work. I can't do it for you, but I can tell you that you're capable of change. Everyone is. Imagine a bedroom stuffed with clothes and videos, one wall taken up by a desk piled high with work and bills and the floor littered with kids' toys. You'd take one look at that bedroom and know that the couple who slept there couldn't have a great sex life. I always say that the bedroom is the emotional center of your house, and has to be clutter-free if you want to feel rested and capable of love. Well, the same is true for your relationship with your partner. This is the primary emotional relationship in your life. It sets the tone for all your other relationships. It can bring you the greatest love and joy in your life, or it can weigh you down and suffocate you. Don't get trapped by your own mess. Climb out. Work through it little by little. The rewards are well worth any effort it may take.

Live in the present

People hang on to clutter because they're clinging to the past or fantasizing about the future. I tell them to live in the present—to keep the clothes, furniture, books, papers, and other belongings that make sense for the life they are living now. In the same way, when I asked you to create a vision for your ideal relationship, I didn't intend for you to rip a photo of George Clooney or Jennifer Aniston out of a magazine. An ideal relationship doesn't mean an upgrade. (And—I don't mind being the one to break it to you: Clooney? Aniston? It ain't gonna happen!)

Be realistic about the past

For better or worse, people change. In the early days of your relationship, your partner may have put on the charm, wooing you with sweet nothings, surprise gifts, and honeymoon sex. Call me a cynic, but people can't court forever; everyday life gets in the way. Besides—it would get boring. Don't cling to the early days of your relationship, hoping they will reemerge. Don't harbor resentment if (to paraphrase Neil Diamond) your partner stops bringing you flowers and writing you love songs. Keep the relationship real—let it grow and flourish in the here and now. There's nothing wrong with trying to revitalize romance, but let the past be what it is: a happy memory.

Be realistic about the future

Living in the present means facing your problems head-on instead of running away in hope of finding something better. Many of us grew up with parents who divorced or have watched our friends and family go through divorce. It is hard to watch your loved ones go through that upheaval and pain. Somewhere in the back of your mind, did you get used to the idea that relationships end and come to believe that when the going gets tough, it's time to get going? Remember that every long-term relationship has its share of rough spots and sometimes the only thing that gets you through them is knowing that you're committed for the long haul. Even when the present isn't your ideal, you have faith that somehow the fog will clear so you're going to persevere *no matter what*. The point is to be realistic about the future. Don't bail on a relationship that hits a rough patch because you think a new one will necessarily be better. It rarely is and chances are you will carry the clutter from one relationship to the other and set the new one up to fail, too.

Why do people repeat the same mistakes in relationship after relationship? Change is hard. It's hard for you to change, even if you want to. But here is a fundamental truth—the only person you can change is yourself. Period. And it's impossible to make your partner change until she sees the reason to do so and embraces that. Change for her won't just happen—no matter how much you want it. I have been told so many times by one partner that they knew of the other's clutter tendencies before they started living together, but felt that they could change that person. Consider this, if you're struggling and hoping you can change something you don't like about your mate, you can't. Forget it! The only person you can reliably change is yourself.

Face fears

Some relationships do and should end. You're committed enough to be reading this book, which means you're willing to put in the work your relationship needs. But sometimes that's not enough.

Dear Peter:

I hate confrontation, and I have a deep-seated feeling of not deserving anything, so I stay in this marriage because I feel trapped, kind of the way I feel trapped by all of my stuff. I have been trying to work on the marriage for a long time, but I am really starting to feel like I get to have some expectations from him, and with that comes needing to have expectations from myself. This includes my clutter obviously, and then actually living the way I want to. I am afraid that my husband won't fit into that picture that is clutter-free, peaceful, and calm.

Is your partner committed?

Commitment comes in different shapes and forms. Not everyone is comfortable sitting down for a heart-to-heart or admitting his or her faults. So don't misread discomfort, hesitation, or exhaustion for lack of commitment. But do look into your heart for the right answer. Love is critical to a relationship's survival, but love isn't always enough. Here are some questions to ask yourself. This is not a quiz, and your relationship doesn't need a perfect score to work, but these questions can help illuminate what you probably already know in your heart.

These are questions with potentially painful answers and it might be helpful to use the answers to open the dialogue with your partner. At some point, when the answers are bleak and you're not at all sure of your partner's commitment, you have to ask yourself: "Are you in this relationship for the right reasons?"

Activity
Questions to Explore Your
Partner's Commitment

When you've answered these questions about yourself, try answering them from your partner's perspective and see how they might perceive you—it can be eye-opening.

Does your partner try to make you happy? How?

Do you believe that your partner is genuinely "in" this relationship as an active participant? What evidence do you see of this?

Does your relationship fall where it should on your partner's list of priorities? What examples show this?

Is your partner willing to do what it takes—to genuinely try to break habits and change behaviors—to restore peace and happiness to your household? In what ways is he/she trying?

Can you live with the faults that your partner won't change? What are those faults?

The fears that keep you in a relationship

Fear is a form of clutter. Fear of loneliness, fear of failure, low self-esteem. Sometimes the easiest thing to do in a relationship is nothing. Rather than work hard to connect with and engage, we default to "the easy" option of coasting because it is easier to stay in than to get out. Are you staying in your relationship because you're afraid of being alone? Are you afraid to admit that the promises you made, the hopes you nurtured, and the work you invested in a lifetime partnership were all for nothing? I don't blame you. Being alone is hard, and there are very few people who prefer it to being in a less-than-ideal relationship. Admitting failure to yourself is hard enough. Admitting it to your fam-

ily, friends, and colleagues in the form of a separation or divorce is only harder. And even if you don't have issues with low self-esteem, a breakup is a big blow. It's normal to fear that you won't find someone else, that you're not attractive enough, that there must be something wrong with you if this didn't work out. But there is more than enough evidence out there proving that leaving the wrong relationship is empowering. It makes you stronger, clearer, and lighter. The weight and clutter that impede you falls away, and you rediscover who you are and what life you want to live.

I want you to be honest with yourself about what you're settling for and why. Take a good, hard look at the person in front of you. At the end of the relationship or the end of your life (whichever comes first), will you regret the time you spent with this person? If so, it's time to take that scary leap into the unknown. Remember what I say about the junk that crowds people's houses: Does stuff help you create the life you want? If you don't love it, get rid of it. You know if you're in a bad relationship. You know if you're not being treated fairly or with respect. Ask for what you need. Have patience and faith. Weather rough patches. But don't choose daily humiliation and suffering because you're afraid of the unknown. Respect yourself enough to be alone, even lonely. And be grateful for the Internet, which can guarantee you some dates (of varying quality) within twenty-four hours.

Other relationships

If a romantic relationship isn't working out, you break up. But what do you do when another relationship no longer brings you the pleasure and satisfaction it once did? Friendships, family relationships, and work relationships can be intense and emotional or light and easy. They can be boring or draining. A bad friendship can be just as cluttered and unhealthy for you as a bad partner.

We all have some relationships that we carry on for the wrong reasons. Sometimes it's inertia. Sometimes you stick with a friend just because you've been friends for so long. Sometimes you stay with them out of habit, because you don't want to be lonely, because you're avoiding conflict—many of the same reasons people stay in bad relationships. But holding on to an unhealthy relationship just because you've known the person forever is the same mistake that people make when they stuff their garages or basements with useless memorabilia from their pasts. Live in the present. Get rid of the stuff that you no longer honor and respect.

How should you end a friendship that is draining you? Do you end it dramatically, by telling your friend it isn't working for you? Or do you stop returning e-mails and phone calls, passively allowing yourself to fall out of touch? In the end it doesn't matter how you do it; if you've lost interest in a friendship, don't waste your time. *Let it go.* Be thoughtful, though, it is always best to handle ending any relationship with the kind of care that you would like extended to you in the same circumstance. I realize this can be painful for both of you and you should be prepared, because even if it wasn't a great friendship you will definitely feel a loss. But when the time is right, heave ho. Life is short and you need

Dear Peter:
I do seem to manage my relationships just like my material things; I streamline. I keep few but solid friendships. To me, this is exactly the same as keeping few but meaningful collectibles or few but useful pieces of furniture. I know people who have tons of acquaintances but don't nurture their relationships, and I feel that is the same as people who acquire "just-in-case" stuff and don't use it.

to make choices that enrich and fulfill your life, not keep it cluttered.

Celebrate successes

As I mentioned, it's tough if not impossible to recapture the giddy joy of a new relationship. But part of your job as half of a couple is to try your hardest to find happiness, and happiness takes work. You need to create time to enjoy and appreciate each other. Take interest in each other's lives. All too quickly, a relationship can settle into a routine and you find yourselves doing the same thing together night after night. If that's staring at the TV while you wolf down fast food, I can guarantee that your days will blur together into boredom. You'll have no memories to see you through harder times (and, eventually, your old age). Take walks together. Socialize. Try new things. We are told constantly to invest in our retirement plans and how critical they are for security and happiness in our old age. The same is true for memories and shared experiences. Invest energy into your relationship or you won't see returns.

Relationships are intangible. You can't look in the mirror and say, "Wow, this relationship is clutter-free," or "Boy, has this relationship lost weight!" When you work together to improve your relationship, when you make changes, when you feel that things are better, be sure to acknowledge them. Celebration makes things that are hard to measure tangible and celebrations become memories of shared experience, so be sure to take the time to celebrate yourselves.

In some religious traditions, the community celebrations that are common are centered on events called sacraments—christenings, marriages, communion. The definition of a sacra-

ment in this context is "an external sign of an interior reality"— that is, a ceremony has developed as a way for the community to celebrate or show publicly what they believe is happening at a faith level—a community celebration to mark a faith-based experience. It's a really wonderful concept—an external sign of an interior reality. Ask yourself what the "interior reality" of your relationship is. What special bond or union do you and your partner enjoy? How are your souls connected? Then ask how others looking at you would see evidence of that truth. How do you show the "interior reality" of your relationship to the world?

Celebrate what you have and what you are developing. Talk about the changes you've successfully made and use successes you've already achieved as the groundwork for more changes. Acknowledge yourselves for the work you have done and the joy you are creating in a shared life together.

And then there's the stuff . . .

We've talked about clearing the mental clutter that interferes with your relationship, but what about the physical clutter? Physical clutter also takes its toll. If the space that you and your partner share is cluttered and both of you are fine with that, great. I'm all for shared happiness. But if the weight of your stuff is weighing on one or both of you, it's critical to get it under control. Which comes first—the clutter or the problems? As far as I'm concerned, it's a chicken-and-egg issue. What I can tell you is that physical clutter and relationship problems seem to go hand in hand, and I don't believe you can fix one without fixing the other. Getting rid of the physical clutter is, as they say, another story, and it's one I've already told in my book *It's All Too Much: An Easy Plan for Living a Richer Life with Less Stuff*. I'll just boil it down to the basics.

Dear Peter,

Thank you for your appearance on *Oprah* last week. You said something that really changed the dynamic in the home I share with my hoarder husband.

You said that you will never win an argument about stuff with a hoarder. You are so right. I never have and it has made me feel like a loser for years. He was always saying that I didn't ask him "right" or making some other excuse. What a master manipulator!

I feel like a ten-ton weight has been lifted off of me and I am practically tingling with happiness. I even cleaned out a folder I had been avoiding for months. You see, I felt so bad, I started doing it, too. The difference is that I see the junk and he doesn't.

His problem has driven a wedge between us. I don't know where you go from here. He says he puts me first, but the evidence is otherwise. I do so want to find happiness in my own home.

The clutter-clearing process I use is consistent across emotional and physical clutter:

- Create a vision for the life you want and the space you share with your partner. Every item in that space should contribute to your vision.
- Overcome obstacles that prevent you from letting go of items. It doesn't matter if it was expensive or if you might need it one day. If it doesn't serve the vision you have for this life you want, it has to go.

- Commit time to clearing the clutter, even if it's only twenty minutes and two garbage bags every day. If you stop making purchases and purge a small area of your home daily for twenty minutes, you'll be surprised at how quickly you start to see changes.
- Communicate with your partner about your shared vision. If you aren't both agreed and committed, you won't succeed.
- Set boundaries and respect limits. You can only have as many books as you have feet of bookshelf space. The same is true for clothes, collections, hobbies, holiday decorations, bathroom supplies, and so on. Boundaries and limits are critical for a healthy and balanced relationship.
- Make changes. Only by changing the role stuff plays in your life will you be able to stop buying more things and let go of the clutter that impedes your life.
- Live in the present. Don't hold on to memories that take up so much room that you can't live your life. Don't hold on to an inordinate amount of stuff in hope of preparing for a range of possible futures. Your life right now is the priority. Fix it.
- Face fears. Sometimes clearing away the clutter forces you to face very hard truths about yourself and your relationship. Don't hide behind your stuff. Get rid of it and face the bare truth.
- Celebrate successes. As you clear stuff away, you will feel lighter, as if you can breathe again. Enjoy this together. This is your life.

2

Work

To-dos . . . or not to-dos? That is the question.

My job requires me to travel frequently and I get to see the inside of more airports than I care to remember. About six months ago I was checking in for a flight and the airline employee behind the counter was shockingly abrupt and aggressive. She ignored my initial friendly hello, avoided eye contact, and met my question about the delayed departure time with a very abrupt "I'm too busy to have that information, check the departure board!" When I asked another question about a possible upgrade, she flung my boarding pass onto the counter and it fell to the floor.

It takes a lot to rattle me, so I took the most direct course of action. In a calm, pleasant voice I said to the woman, "I'm really confused here. I have been nothing but polite and courteous and you have been incredibly rude in return. Have I done something to offend or upset you?" The shock on the woman's face was clear—as was her regret. It turned out she had dealt with a number of really difficult and rude passengers before me and that experience had really affected her mood. I left the ticket counter on good terms with the employee—she was even smiling—but the experience really reinforced something for me.

Like it or not, most of us spend a good chunk of our waking hours on the job. Earning a paycheck to support ourselves is part of life. Work can be enjoyable and challenging or a horrendous drudgery. But no matter what your work conditions, you should regularly take stock of your job situation. Work is not life, and you should not get sucked into the clutter of work or let the clutter of your work overrun your life.

We can't all experience one-hundred-percent job satisfaction every hour of every day. Nor can we expect to be endlessly talented, duly rewarded, and regularly promoted. At the same time, life is meant to be lived, and not just in the hours before and after you punch the clock. What I'm talking about here is this old adage: Do you live to work or work to live? The ideal job is fulfilling and engaging (as opposed to soul-draining); it provides you with enough money to live; and it paves the way for greater future opportunities should you desire them. No matter what you do or where you stand in your career, you have the power to determine your own path. The choices you make every day at work will, in the end, add up to a sizable chunk of your lifetime achievement.

For some of us, work is often a second home, so like your home, work should be a place where form follows function. Just as your bedroom is the emotional center of your home and your kitchen is the place that provides nourishment for your family, your workplace should be the center of productivity. It should be a place where you feel inspired and energized, at your intellectual best.

But work can get cluttered. Not just physically—emotionally. How do you feel when you think about the mountain of tasks that face you on any given day? Are you anxious and overwhelmed?

Have the everyday challenges of work grown out of control, taking on a life of their own? Do you hate the field you work in but feel powerless to change? Are your relationships with colleagues bogged down with extraneous baggage? If your working life is stalled or unfulfilling, stressful or financially insufficient, it's time to clean up the clutter and find your path again. Let's get started.

Quiz
Is Your Work Life Cluttered?

1. On Sunday nights, knowing a new work week is about to begin, how do you feel?
    a. *Energized from the weekend.*
    b. *A little bummed that the weekend is over.*
    c. *A looming sense of dread.*

2. If you had to start all over again:
    a. *I'd follow the same career path.*
    b. *I'd make some different decisions, but my goals would be the same.*
    c. *I'd find a career that matched my interests.*

3. Your job isn't perfect:
    a. *But I know it's the right career move for me.*
    b. *But it's money in the bank.*
    c. *But I have no other options.*

4. If you stay in this job:
    a. I'm in line for a promotion.
    b. I hope to move up eventually.
    c. I'll be doing the same thing for the rest of my life.

5. At the end of a long work day, how do you feel?
    a. Tired but fulfilled.
    b. Exhausted, but I'll survive.
    c. Just plain over it.

6. Outside of your job, how would you describe your life?
    a. Hectic, but mostly satisfying.
    b. A juggling act that I barely pull off.
    c. Nonexistent.

7. What is most true about the people you work with?
    a. I like spending time with them, even outside the office.
    b. I respect them, even if they're not my best friends.
    c. They are making my life a living hell.

8. How would you describe your desk?
    a. Functional and neat.
    b. Messy, but I know where things are for the most part.
    c. The Mount Everest of paperwork.

9. How does the idea of another year at this job make you feel?
    a. Accepting.
    b. Resigned.
    c. Ill.

10. The amount you get paid:
    a. *Seems fair for the work I do.*
    b. *Is never quite enough.*
    c. *Is completely unreasonable given how hard I work.*

Is your work life cluttered?

If your answers are mostly As:
I'm guessing you know this already, but you're in pretty good shape. You may not love every moment of your work, but you find it rewarding and know you're on the right track. Congratulations! That's more than plenty of people can say. Keep working hard and with a sense of purpose, and take control of your own career. You'll move onward and upward.

If your answers are mostly Bs:
Well, this may not be the perfect job, but what is? How do you know whether to accept "less than ideal," or if you should move on? You can always look for greener pastures, but the first step is trying to improve your current situation. Use the tools I'll give you to fine-tune your work life. And make sure you evaluate your options frequently, keeping your end goals in mind.

If your answers are mostly Cs:
You're done. This isn't the way to live your life—feeling doomed to toil in some dead-end job until the end of time. You should change your path and you can, starting now.

Imagine the career you want

How did you get where you are? Why this job? Plenty of people land a job right out of school and stay in it. Maybe you got promoted, got a new job, got promoted again, and now, before you know it, ten years have passed and your job isn't particularly fulfilling, but you don't feel like you can start all over again. Did you choose your job or did your job choose you? Do you work in a family business? Did your parents pressure you into a certain job or career? Do you have a fantasy career that you've never pursued? Do you feel stuck in a job you don't like because you have to provide for your family? Do you regret never going to school to acquire skills for your dream job or to get a higher degree to increase your options? Do you like your chosen field but have troubled relationships with your boss or colleagues? Has a job that you love become all-encompassing so that other parts of your life (relationships, family, health, spirituality) are suffering?

The first step toward decluttering your work life is to think about what you want from your career. Notice that I use the word "career," not "job." A job is work that you take to earn money to live. A career is work in a certain field that you undertake over a significant portion of your life, with opportunities for development and advancement. If you don't like your job, the advice is easy: Get a different one. You don't like your boss? Find a job with a nicer boss. You want more money? Ask for a raise. There are a million books that will tell you how. But when it comes to building a career, the game is much more complex. Your expectations for what you'll give, and what you'll get in return, are much higher. Remember the basic question I keep returning to:

What is the life I want to live?

I'm not asking you, "What is the career you want?" and there's a reason. I'm trying to encourage you to look at your life as a whole. Your relationship with your mate isn't your life. Your career isn't your life. Your family isn't your life. But each of these adds up to your life. It's impossible to quantify how important each of these elements is and so every day of your life is spent balancing them to some extent.

In a commencement address at Georgia Tech in the '90s, Brian Dyson, then CEO of Coca-Cola, offered the following: "Imagine life as a game in which you are juggling five balls in the air. You name them: Work. Family. Health. Friends. Spirit. And you're keeping all of these in the air. You will soon understand that work is a rubber ball. If you drop it, it will bounce back. But the other four balls—family, health, friends, and spirit—are made of glass. If you drop one of these, they will be irrevocably scuffed, marked, nicked, damaged, or even shattered. They will never be the same."

This modern-day parable emphasizes the resilience of work when compared to the fragility of health and relationships. And yet time and again, it's our preoccupation with our work that creates most stress and anxiety in our lives. Are you able to strike a balance between your work and the other important areas of your life? How good are you at juggling the competing demands and responsibilities of each? Do you keep in mind the "bounciness" of work—how you can take greater risks without losing it forever?

When you imagine your ideal life, what part does work play? Now remember, saying you want to be a movie star or a hedge fund billionaire doesn't get us anywhere. Given your abilities and inclination, what goals are reasonable? Let me help you get started.

- **Money**

Well, obviously. If we didn't need money, plenty of us would consider not working at all. What I want you to consider is the role money plays in creating your ideal life. The work you do pays for the life you live. Have you cut yourself a good deal? In other words, is the life you have worth the work you do to pay for it?

What is your financial situation? Are you in the habit of living beyond your means? Are you living paycheck to paycheck? Are you in debt? Are you successfully saving for your retirement? Are your work decisions influenced by the need to meet obligations—from credit card bills to mortgages to child care?

- **Day-to-day fulfillment**

How much pleasure do you get out of your work? If your job doesn't pay the bills, I sure hope you love what you do. Do you feel intellectually, emotionally, or physically stimulated by your work in a positive way? Are you doing something good for yourself or others? Is it fun? Do you enjoy being around your coworkers or clients? Does work bring you satisfaction?

- **Work/life balance**

How does work fit into your life? Does it leave you with enough free time to enjoy your friends, family, and romantic life? Do you need to set boundaries in order to protect your home life from your work life (or vice versa)? If so, will your work—your boss or your clients or you yourself—respect those boundaries?

- **Long-term growth**

How long will you be happy at your current job? Is it in a field that will interest you for the foreseeable future? Are there opportunities for growth where you work? Are you developing skills

Activity
Define Your Vision for Your Career

Take a moment to think about the work you do now—what you like about it, what you find rewarding, and what you'd like to change. Imagine, also, your ideal career. With these thoughts in mind, complete the following table.

What do you like about the job you currently have?

Words that describe the career you want to have:

- _____

- _____

- _____

- _____

- _____

- _____

What skills do you have and want to use in your work?

What skills do you want to develop?

Describe how your ideal career would unfold:

What can you change to make the ideal career path emerge?

and experience that will benefit you in your next job and the job after that? Does this job represent a stepping-stone toward where you want your career to go?

Clear the clutter of unreal expectations

My work has put me on *The Oprah Winfrey Show* more than once. It's something I really love, but believe me, no job is all glamour. I help clear some of the most cluttered houses in the country, which means digging through basements full of boxes and garages that can best be described as black holes of clutter. Those boxes don't just hide the floor—they hide mildew, rodents, mold, and other unspeakable nastiness. If you don't believe me, speak to my dermatologist or some of the crew who've seen me gag more than once! Every job has its dull, dirty, back-breaking, mind-numbing moments. If you aren't prepared to get your hands dirty, chances are you won't go very far.

Just because you have a goal doesn't mean you can get there right away. It takes time and effort. Remember that you have to work for what you want. Nobody's going to hand you free money unless you win the lottery. Nobody's going to look into your eyes and decide you deserve more responsibility or a promotion. You have to earn them. Nobody's going to give you a raise as a birthday present. So no more sitting on your butt in silent resentment. Clarify your goals first and then we can talk about how to achieve them.

Watch out for obstacles

Problems at work can be small—the guy in the cubicle next to you cuts his nails with noisy clippers—or large—your boss has

Dear Peter:

I am a very organized person when it comes to my space and also to planning. But this is most likely my biggest obstacle in getting to achieve my goals. I spend so much time planning, thinking, and getting motivated, but when it comes to taking action, I fall short. I would love to be able to just do it, instead of staying in the "getting ready" section. This especially applies to my business and getting it off the ground.

systematically promoted everyone but you. But when it comes to landing a job and growing a career, we all face many of the same obstacles.

Bad communication

Communication is critical to any career. How can you do a good job if you haven't made sure you know exactly what is expected of you? How can you manage others if you don't clearly communicate what is expected of them? Communicating in the workplace isn't about winning or losing. It's not about dragging up past conflicts or talking over people. In this chapter, we'll talk about how to communicate productively in, across, up, and down at your workplace.

No personal goals

The daily grind. It's easy to get caught up in the everyday clutter of a job and lose track of your ultimate goals for this job, for your career, and for your life. Do you want to be your own boss? Do you want to start your own company? Are you simply looking for a job where you like your colleagues, or where you have a certain measure of independence? Your inbox is overflowing with paper or e-mails, or your phone rings off the hook. You have twenty schoolchildren clamoring for your attention or six legal cases to research simultaneously or four impatient customers all wanting attention now! But there is always an end goal, not just for your daily life and your career path, but for the job itself. What is your role in the bigger picture at your company of employ? No matter what your job, if you don't keep your goals in mind, you'll always be Sisyphus, the king in Greek mythology who was condemned to push a boulder up a hill only to watch it roll down, to push it up and watch it roll down again and again throughout eternity.

Cluttered vision

When it comes to work, you need to have an organized vision of what you want to achieve. What is the purpose of your job? If you work for a company, how does your job fit into the company's goals? And what do you want from this job in terms of moving you down your career path?

Poor time management

Just because you're skilled at your job doesn't mean you're good at managing your time. Do you do the most important projects first? Are you easily distracted? Do e-mails or news items suck you away from the task at hand? Do you spend work hours doing personal stuff, like paying bills, planning vacations, or organizing your kids' lives? How much of the day do you spend complaining about your job, relationship, mother-in-law, or children? Is work your social hub—do you spend more time chatting than working? Do you finish one project before picking up the next? Do you procrastinate? Do you spend hours surfing the Web? These may seem like small breaks that improve your day, but what toll are they taking on your career goals?

No boundaries

Sometimes it can seem like your time is out of your control. It can be, if you don't set boundaries. My client Ellen has a friend who calls her at work three or four times a week, expecting to chat for at least half an hour. Ellen, who works for a high-profile businessman, doesn't have time for these calls, but she doesn't want to hurt her friend's feelings. "I don't know what to do," she told me. "I can't say to her, 'Sorry, but we can't be everyday friends. We can only be once-a-week friends.' " Now that e-mails pop into your inbox or onto your handheld at all hours of the day, it's hard to resist taking a peek and firing off a quick reply. When does your workday end? Do you keep the time and emotions of work separate from the time and emotions of home? If not, what impact does that have on your vision for your ideal life?

Inability to manage up

Is your boss clear about his or her expectations? Does she dump work on you without telling you how to prioritize it? Does he have unrealistic expectations for how long a project will take? Are you too confused, busy, or intimidated to ask for clarification? It's not so hard to tell the people below you what to do, but managing up is a critical skill that makes your job easier and sets you up for promotion.

Fear of change

There are many good reasons to change jobs: you've outgrown the work; the commute is killing you; your boss is an inhuman slime. But staying in a bad or dull job is much the same as staying in an unhealthy relationship. Most of us prefer a known evil to the scary unknown, but it's just not healthy or productive for us to be weighed down by that clutter of fear. For some, it might come back to whether this is the career you truly imagine for yourself. Did you choose your job or did your job choose you? If you find yourself complaining, day in and day out, about where you work and what you do, then it's time to embark on a job search. You're right to be conservative—nobody wants those paychecks to stop without a new job lined up—but if you let fear guide your career, what is the cost? You miss out on the growth and stimulation that make work interesting (and keep your paycheck growing!) and create unhappiness and stress in your life when you don't have to.

Activity
What's Getting in the Way of My Ideal Career?

Reviewing the sections above, write down the obstacles that stand in the way of landing the career you want.

- _____

- _____

- _____

Declutter your career

It's impossible to live the life you want in a home that is cluttered. Your home reflects your state of mind. If you want to be happy, peaceful, inspired, and loving, your home has to have all those characteristics. Likewise, like it or not, your career defines you. It's close to impossible to spend more than ten minutes with a group of new people before someone asks you what you do. You spend at least eight hours a day toiling away at your job, so it's worth making those hours stimulating, intellectually rewarding, financially beneficial, and even fun. If you're not happy in your job, you are spending your days working not only for someone else, but also against yourself. That is time and energy you can never recover. When you work for someone else, and most of us

Dear Peter:

I work out of my home. My inability to create a real process for work filing, note taking, in/out needs, had completely spilled over into my life. How can I justify an hour at the gym—taking care of me—when my desk is in complete disarray? How can I know that I don't have something due or a phone call about to come in when I don't have a system? And, if I don't know if something is going to happen, how can I be away from my desk to go to the gym? It's a complete vicious cycle. When my desk is cluttered, I have a difficult time really thinking through the project that I'm on. I start at the computer, and see the mess out of the corner of my eye, which completely distracts me. I then have to stop working to deal with the mess, which puts me behind on my deadlines. Without all the clutter, I feel focused, in charge, and unstoppable.

do, it can feel like you have little control over your work life. But I hope as you work through this section, you'll realize that just as you can purge clutter and reclaim your home, so can you clear out the physical and emotional clutter in your work life to take back control of your workday and your career.

Commit time

Of all the sections of this book, cleaning up your career may be the decluttering process that takes the longest. Why? Because experience can't be gained overnight; finding the right next step is a slow and deliberate process; and proving yourself in a job takes years. No matter what, you're probably destined to spend years of your life punching that time clock, so invest the time to clear a clean, straight path to your career goals.

Time to rethink your current job

You can't just stride into the office on a Monday morning with a pencil behind your ear and magically transform yourself into a dream employee. Your new resolve might give you the energy to get a lot done over the next few days, and that's great, but in all likelihood you'll slip back into old habits in a week or so. Organization is not so much something you do as something you are. Decluttering only works if you make it a way of life. You need to learn how to make choices based on your priorities. That's why I want you to approach this methodically.

Time to explore options for the future

The best career moves don't happen in the heat of the moment. You'll have to spend time thinking about your goals, researching the paths to get there, and improving yourself as a candidate. What new areas or positions interest you? Start with an open

mind, exploring any and everything that has ever sounded fun or inspiring. When you have an idea of what sort of change you might want to make, consider your skill set. What jobs can you get with the knowledge and experience you currently have? Do you have the skills you need to be in the field or position that interests you? Only after you've done preliminary self-exploration and research can you begin to make changes that will move you closer to where you want to be.

Time to clean up your act

Improving your work life isn't as simple as having a clean desk. But what can I say? I do this for a living—it's a good place to start. There's no faster way to inspire an immediate change in attitude than with an uncluttered, clear, pristine desk. It's a little like making your bed. A made bed anchors a room, sets the tone for the day, says, "I respect my space," and shows a commitment to routines and organization. So you are your desk. If it's cluttered, how are you supposed to prioritize? How can you be efficient? Think of your desk as a reflection of your head. No matter how creative and brilliant you are, I can assure you that you'll perform better with an organized desk. Now let's get to it. Here's how.

Activity
Quick Desk Purge

1. File. You shouldn't have anything on your desk that isn't "active," meaning it still needs to be dealt with. Filing isn't complex, and it isn't high priority, which is why a "to file" pile tends to grow high. Get rid of those piles immediately, even if it takes you an hour. If you take ten minutes to file at the end of the day, you'll always be able to keep

your desk clean. Filing and tidying up at the end of the day is a good way to decompress before you go home, as well as a way to clarify and reinforce what you did today and what you need to do tomorrow.

2. Get rid of the miniature Zen garden. After you've filed, clear your workspace of anything that you don't use regularly. If you must have sentimental items and toys (really, must you?), pare them down to a bare minimum. This isn't a high school locker. You're a grown-up and a professional. Your desk should reflect that. The same goes for the stuffed animals, Vegas souvenirs, and collectible action figures!

3. Use a vertical file organizer for "active" files. Reserve your inbox for items that need to be dealt with pronto. For ongoing projects, create files and store them in an easily accessible desktop file organizer or a rolling file cart that slips easily under your desk and can be accessed quickly and efficiently.

4. Create systems that work. No matter if you're a shoe salesman, a full-time dad, or a rock star, you'll do your job better if you have fool-proof systems in place.

- When you listen to your phone messages, the calls you need to return should always be written down in the same place.
- When you plan a meeting, a playdate, or a concert in Madison Square Garden, the event goes immediately into a calendar.
- When you pay a bill, complete a sale, or finish an album, all documentation should immediately be filed away.
- Keep a running to-do list on a notepad or electronically. Start a new page every day, copying outstanding to-dos onto the new page. When you complete a task, check it off and note the date.

> You'll always know exactly when you got something done and have a clear record in case you need to refer back to it.

And so on. Take notes. Keep a calendar. Return calls. Log important addresses and phone numbers. Be accountable. You know how there are some ultrareliable people you trust to do what they said they'd do, when they said they'd do it? You can be one of those people. Your organized desk is the first step and says "I mean business" to everyone who sees it.

Communicate

Almost none of us works alone. Now that you've done the quick purge of your desk, it's time to turn your attention to some of the tougher messes. Even if you have a perfectly pleasant relationship with your boss and/or your underlings, if you're not getting the results you want—if you aren't satisfied with your career and the progress you're making—then you need to declutter and focus your communication.

> Dear Peter:
> There really is a true connection to throwing off the chains of clutter and the way we feel about our lives and our space. I discovered recently that if I set aside some time before leaving for work to purge and organize an area, all day long people compliment my appearance, saying, "There's something different about you today!" It seems that cleaning up that clutter is almost more effective on our minds, bodies, and souls than two hours at the salon!

Manage up and down

Your communication with your boss shouldn't be dramatically different from your interactions with your peers or subordinates. Of course, there are power dynamics, but certain elements should be consistent: respect, professionalism, and clarity of expectations.

Be a team player. No matter what the hierarchy, think of yourself as a team member. You're working to help your boss do her job. You're working to help your employees do their jobs. Nobody is a better person than anyone else—people just have differing levels of experience, skill, and responsibility. If you aren't being treated with the respect you deserve, don't stoop to their level. Maintain your dignity. Stay your ground and calmly say, "I'm happy to address your concerns. Can you sit down and talk this through?" (If your boss is a monster like Meryl Streep's Miranda Priestley in *The Devil Wears Prada*, who would fire you for merely suggesting a calm discussion, then you have a choice to make: accept the abuse or start shopping your résumé around.)

Set your own goals. If your boss isn't clear about how you should be spending your time, how he or she wants something done, or what the priorities are, instead of waiting for direction, take some initiative. Tell your boss what you think the priorities are based on the company's business goal, articulate how that affects your work, and ask for affirmation of your plan. Once you've set goals and had them approved, go out and achieve them.

Ask forgiveness, not permission. Often a boss is thrilled to have employees who forge ahead with their ideas. Most of the time these supervisors would rather an independent-minded employee make a few mistakes than ask permission before reloading paper in the fax machine. But use caution when setting your own rules. Get a sense of the workplace culture and take your cue from that. If your boss isn't onboard with this philosophy, you can get yourself in real trouble.

Separate work and friendship. In this day and age, the social line between boss and worker is fuzzy. As colleagues, you spend so much time together that friendship often develops. No matter which position you have—higher or lower—don't let the friendship interfere with your performance. Even if your boss is your friend, she still calls the shots. And even if you love going out for beers with your employee, you can still require that he show up on time with no performance-hampering hangover.

Report on your efforts. If a boss is inaccessible, the best way to stay in touch (and cover your ass) is to prepare regular status reports that show what projects you are working on and what progress you've made. Again, this makes your boss's job easier. Instead of trying to keep track of everything you're doing and asking about it whenever he remembers, he can always look it up, have the latest information, and react when it's convenient for him.

Stay on topic
Clear out the clutter of long meetings and unfocused discussions. Communication without purpose is a total waste of time in the workplace. Meetings without an agenda, without a time limit, and without action minutes are pretty much a waste of time. Almost every productive workplace discussion could be defined by the following talking points:

1. Here is where we are now.
2. Here is where we want to be.
3. Here is how I think we can get there.

Listen to and respect others' ideas
Remember, it isn't important to "win." Your focus should be on getting the job done in the most efficient way possible. Talking

over someone else, no matter how annoying they are, is a surefire way to spur them on . . . and on and on.

Acknowledge and exclude emotions
No matter how much time you spend at the office, you have to remember that this is your job. It's not your family, and it's not a love affair. You don't have to like everyone you deal with and you don't have to be happy with every decision that gets made. If you do disagree with a decision that impacts you or your ability to do your work, it's fine to say so, but keep it quick, clean, and unemotional.

Document as much as you need to in order to guarantee results
Nobody hates excess paperwork more than I do. But clear and precise documentation is a valuable part of communicating in the workplace. If you have a boss who is too busy to meet with you, send him a weekly status update (electronically, if possible). That way he can check up on what you've been doing when he has time for it. If you're ever in a situation where your performance is challenged, you have documentation of how thorough you have been—and you've given your boss every opportunity to help you improve your performance along the way. Documentation is one way of tracking your progress and a tool to protect yourself, should you ever need it.

Request performance evaluations and translate criticisms
into action points
If there is room to move up the ladder at your current job, be sure you can expect a performance review. It's important for your boss to take the time to evaluate your work, sit down with you to assess it, and offer suggestions for improvement. Performance evaluation is critical to help you keep on track and feel confident that

your contribution is noted and valued. If you're not being evaluated, how can you ever be promoted?

If and when your boss or anyone else at work offers criticisms, never defend yourself on the spot. Say, "I appreciate the feedback. Let me absorb it overnight before I respond." Always sleep on criticism. The next day, if you feel the comment was fair, address how you plan to improve and ask whether that response is what your boss was looking for. If you disagree with the criticism, respond professionally, citing examples of contradicting behavior and refer to the documentation that has become a part of your normal work practice.

Set boundaries

Remember my mantra: You only have the space you have! You can only have as many shoes as you have feet of space in your closet. Similarly, you only have so many hours in the day. You can devote all of your waking hours to work if work is the most important thing to you. Or you can set limits that protect you and your personal life from your work. The hours you work may seem like a decision over which you have no control, but trust me, you do. As the old cliché goes, no one ever had "I wish I'd spent more hours at work" carved into their tombstone. There is always a way to find a better balance between your job and your life. And there is always another job that is more accommodating. Only you can evaluate your values when it comes to your attachment to this job versus how it infringes on your life. Remember the story of juggling the five balls—this is a fundamental and very healthy balance that each of us must reach.

Balancing work and home life is an ongoing effort for anyone with a career. Even if you manage to leave your place of business at a reasonable hour, it's still hard to shift gears. Whether you're glancing at your cell phone every time it vibrates with incoming e-mail or voicemail or mulling over the day's events in the middle of dinner, being where you are takes work.

Divide your time

Job permitting, establish a fixed time by which you leave work every day. Once you leave, set limits for how work intrudes on your home. Turn off electronic devices. If your boss insists on being able to reach you at all hours, remind her that having time to yourself enables you to do a better job. Discuss and agree upon what constitutes an "emergency" worth interrupting your downtime. This is a key part of managing upward. If you don't establish clear boundaries and insist on respecting them, no one else will.

Quality time

Just because you're home with your family doesn't mean you're *with your family*. Coming home in time to eat dinner with the people you love isn't so meaningful if dinner is constantly interrupted by the phone, e-mail, or text messages. A friend of mine has been struggling in her marriage for several years now. Her husband says he wants the relationship to survive, but the first thing he does every morning, before he even rolls over to say "good morning," before his feet even touch the floor, is check his cell phone and send out a few e-mails. Based on that act alone—something that he could easily do after saying good morning—it's hard for my friend to believe that her husband is remotely interested in improving the marriage. Have clear priorities. Be where you are. Agree with your partner or family to have firm rules for cell phone (or other handheld) usage, and stick to them. The same goes for other forms of multitasking.

Take real vacations

I get into so much debate around the issue of work and holidays in this country. Did you know that according to the Bureau of Labor Statistics, the average American male is now working one hundred more hours every year than his counterpart in the 1970s? Amazingly, the United States is the only first-world economy that doesn't provide workers with guaranteed vacation time. What's that about? My view is simple—it's crazy for someone to have only two weeks paid vacation a year and even crazier that nearly half of American workers don't take all of the vacation days they are owed. Sure, work is important, but vacations are equally valuable. They are important times to recharge, rethink, and clear that work clutter out of your head. Even if you're in a tough financial spot, it's important to take pleasure in life whenever you can. Do whatever it takes to leave your job in good shape when you go. Assign someone to cover you, and leave their name and number on your voicemail and e-mail. Work ahead, if you must. Leave your boss with a status report. Then *go*. Be hard to reach. You think that they can't do without you? The cemetery is full of indispensable people. Enjoy your time off. Spend time with those you love. Go someplace beautiful, even if you can't afford to travel. Take time to make sure you're living the life you want. If you can't manage to let go of work and have a good time on vacation, you need to make real changes.

Prioritize your time

Take a moment to study this sample chart. Assume project A is this worker's priority. Look how much time she devotes to other projects. She doesn't finish project A until Friday morning, but if she had started Monday morning and worked on that project alone, she would have finished in two hours, by 11:00 a.m. Monday morning. Well, obviously. You all know that e-mail and snack breaks are time saps. But it's hard to know how much time you're

Activity
Evaluate Your Time Management

Make a chart similar to this one and keep track of how you spend all of your time at work for three to five days. Note that I've used fifteen-minute increments. Fifteen minutes may seem like a short amount of time, but every minute counts.

	Monday	Tuesday	Wednesday	Thursday	Friday
9:00–9:15	Read newspaper and drink coffee	Read newspaper and drink coffee	Read newspaper and drink coffee	Read newspaper and drink coffee	Staff meeting
9:15–9:30	Checking e-mail	Checking e-mail	Checking e-mail	Checking e-mail	
9:30–9:45			Paying bills	Working on project A	
9:45–10:00		Working on project B	Working on project B		
10:00–10:15	Working on project A	Working on project C			
10:15–10:30		Coffee	Working on project C		
10:30–10:45	Working on project B				Completing project A
10:45–11:00	Working on project A		Coffee		

really losing until you write it out, dissect it, and see where there's clutter in your day.

Once you've made your time chart, pick one or two unnecessary activities that are cluttering your time. You don't have room for them, so—you guessed it—it's time to get rid of them. Prioritizing your time and tasks is a key step in organizing your day.

Make changes

It's time to use your goals to structure your day. It sounds simple, I know, but I can't tell you how often I've listened to people complain about how hard it is to get everything done . . . over a two-hour midweek lunch.

Structure your own day

At work, the most important piece of advice I can give you is to take control of your day. Don't let incoming work control you. Phone calls and e-mail can arrive sounding urgent and demanding immediate attention. Don't let them divert your focus. Trust yourself to decide what gets priority.

Get your e-mail under control

Some major companies have implemented "no e-mail Fridays" to help employees see how much they get done when they're not distracted by the constant influx of e-mail. But e-mail is a critical part of all office jobs and many other occupations. Even if you don't work at a company or aren't part of a group effort, you can take measures to handle your e-mail with maximum efficiency.

1. *Don't become a Pavlovian dog.* Do you respond automatically to that *ping* of incoming e-mail from your computer? Tackle your e-mail in batches. Imagine if you went through your snail mail

one letter at a time throughout the day. You'd pay a bill at noon, renew a magazine subscription at two, and perhaps recycle a flyer an hour later. E-mail trickles in throughout the day, but unless something's urgent or from your boss, you don't have to read or address each e-mail as it arrives. Instead, set aside several times throughout the day—for example: when you arrive, late morning, after lunch, afternoon, and the end of the day. Attack your e-mail at these interludes only, and you'll be amazed at how much you accomplish in between.

2. *Use folders and flags.* Don't let your inbox overflow. Almost all e-mail systems have ways you can add organization to your e-mail in much the same way you organize papers on your desk. Keep the most urgent items—the issues you'll deal with today or this week—in your inbox. Create folders to store e-mail that you need to save for later use or reference. If your program has them, use flags to represent the categories that make the most sense for your job. Mark as unread e-mails you've opened but haven't had time to address.

3. *End conversations.* Unlike most business phone calls, an e-mail exchange can go on far longer than necessary. Cut e-mail exchanges short by signing off with a clear summary of what has been decided.

4. *Translate e-mails to action items.* Some business e-mails share information, in which case they should be read, then filed. The rest generally trigger action items. Someone has to perform an action in order to resolve the problem presented in the e-mail. When you are that someone, the e-mail is a "to-do." Manage your e-mail to-dos by keeping them in your electronic inbox. Or transfer them to an online or paper to-do list where they can more easily be prioritized.

5. *Sometimes e-mail isn't the way to go.* If an e-mail hitting your desktop involves an issue that can be resolved quickly in a conver-

Perfect may not be best

Sometimes the great is the enemy of the good. If you constantly find yourself under incredible pressure to complete tasks and meet deadlines, take a little time to look at how you allocate your time to the job at hand. You may have heard me say that we wear 20 percent of our clothes 80 percent of the time. This 80/20 rule also applies to effort at work. Very often the last 20 percent of a task takes 80 percent of your total time on that task. Never short-change yourself or settle for shoddy work, but seriously consider if a job done perfectly might be killing you, whereas a job well done might be enough.

You are your desk

Earlier you did the Quick Purge of your desk, but the work doesn't stop there. Remember that your desk sends a clear signal about who you are and how you approach your work. You should have an organized desk at the start and finish of every day. Arriving to an organized desk in the morning means that instead of feeling overworked and tired the minute you step into the office, you feel energized and ready to conquer your day.

At the end of each day, straighten up your desk and, if you have unfinished tasks, leave yourself a to-do list to start with first thing in the morning. I promise you that if you transform the clutter in your head into a neat list on a piece of paper, you'll never wake up in the middle of the night stressed about something you forgot to do at work. Yes, the work still has to get done, but being organized and on top of it is the first step to conquering it. Set tomorrow's work mood by spending ten minutes organizing your desk and prioritizing activities before you go home each night.

sation, then pick up the phone and do it. Talking with someone is a great way to build relationships, network a little, and stop an e-mail chain dead in its tracks.

Break work into small, manageable tasks
Don't let yourself get overwhelmed. No matter how insurmountable a task might look, it can be done. Trust me—I've cleared more than seventy-five tons of trash from a single house, and that was just to clear a path to the rooms of clutter. Just set daily, even hourly goals for yourself. Small steps yield big results.

Challenge
Prioritize Your Day

Start every day with a list. Become a person who works methodically. If new tasks crop up during the day, add them to the list in order of priority.

Don't let the urgent take precedence over the important
It's easy to let emergencies or the latest crisis run your day. There are very few truly urgent things in the world (unless you happen to be a transplant surgeon), and if you don't develop the skill of separating the urgent from the important, your job will end up managing you, instead of the other way around. Identify those tasks that most need your attention and don't allow yourself to be easily or unnecessarily distracted. Just because someone puts one of those "high priority" flags on their e-mail doesn't automatically make it so. Prioritize, prioritize, prioritize, and manage your day accordingly.

Personal image

The old advice goes, "Dress for the job you want, not the job you have." This is sound advice, but the real point is that your appearance in the workplace has an impact. It should be obvious that the goal isn't to look attractive so much as it is to look neat, clean, reliable, and professional. Make sure your dress is appropriate for your office by looking to someone whose position and performance you admire.

Personal image goes beyond clothes. How do you comport yourself? Do you bite your nails or chew gum in meetings? If someone walks into your office while you're having a snack, do you continue stuffing a muffin into your mouth as the impromptu meeting proceeds? Do you speak clearly, politely, and respectfully? Do you take personal calls that can be heard across the office? You may wish to be judged on your work alone, but how you behave in the office has an immense impact on how people react to you, and whether and how far your star will rise.

Commitment

Your job is often what you make of it. How seriously do you take your job? Do you go out late at night and drag yourself into work the next day? Can you concentrate on the job at hand or are you sucked into phone calls, blogs, Facebook, or other distractions? Are you the employee whom you'd want to hire if you were the boss? Your commitment, or lack thereof, always comes through. Only by investing in your job will you see real returns.

Make sure your job is doable

If you are organized, efficient, and working a reasonable number of hours per day, then you should be able to perform your job to your own and everyone else's satisfaction. Sure, every job has busier times when you have to put in extra hours, but if you are constantly stretched to the limit, proud of your effort, but still unable to get the work under control, then there is a problem with the job and you need to make a change. Consider the following possibilities:

1. *Your job is too big for one person.* Often, especially if you're a reliable employee, more and more work gets piled on your shoulders. Your boss (or you) is hesitant to hire help, mostly because of the added expense. This is a case of "something's gotta give." Don't just tell your boss you can't do it. Complaining doesn't solve problems. Carve out a logical piece of the job—something discrete that someone else could manage—and ask him to reassign that. Or suggest ways in which your work could be reduced. Remember, if you're a good employee who does the work as well or better than anyone else, your boss shouldn't let you go. She'll respect a valid proposal, and the work you've done to put it together helps her do her job.

2. *Your job is poorly managed.* This is a tough one. You can love your job, but still have a manager who makes your life difficult for one reason or another. This is where managing up comes in.

   a. *Organize.* Make sure that you and your boss define your job the same way by having her sign off on a job description. If your job starts sprawling into other areas (otherwise known as "job creep"), suggest revisiting the job description (and title and compensation, if called for).

   b. *Execute.* Make sure that the work you do fulfills the job description. Stay focused. When your boss pulls you off an assignment or otherwise interferes with your work, be specific and polite about the work you are setting aside to do the new task.

   c. *Report.* Prepare regular reports that show your accomplishments. Include tasks that are incomplete and explanations for why. Take responsibility but don't complain or blame. For example: "I didn't finish the sales reports this month because I was working on the new presentations, which took priority."

3. *You're not the right person for the job.* You know the job isn't getting done. You're overwhelmed and miserable. The easiest route is to blame your boss or the job. The hardest truth to face is that the job isn't right for you. Maybe you don't have the proper skills and need training. Maybe it doesn't play to your strengths. Maybe your interest level isn't high enough to inspire you. The truth may be hard to accept, but you can't make smart decisions about your next move unless you honestly appraise your current situation.

Never quit in a rage

When it comes to your job, don't ever walk out the door in anger. Anger leads to hasty and usually unwise decisions. Don't compound a bad situation with a knee-jerk reaction and a poor choice. Even if you're in the wrong job, you'll almost always do better to launch a job search as an employed person. Take your time. Talk with a trusted coworker who is able to provide you with some honest and objective feedback. Is the problem you or the job? Can the situation be rectified? Do you want it to be rectified or have you decided that it's time for a change? Sometimes we outgrow a job and sometimes a job outgrows us. Don't quit until you have an attractive job offer on paper.

Changing careers

Changing careers is always difficult, especially if you're changing midcareer. You've already invested time developing certain skills. You've made contacts. Maybe you've won hard-earned promotions. But there are also plenty of reasons to make changes. If this isn't the right career for you, why throw good years after bad? Some of my clients want to keep items that clutter their homes because they were expensive. But just because something has value in the world—or once did—doesn't mean it's worth any-

Activity
Career Change Worksheet

Take some time to think about the career you're in. Be aware of what you enjoy, what you find challenging, and what you could do without. Weigh the pros and cons of trying something new and then tackle this table.

Challenges	Benefits
I don't want to start at the bottom and have to work my way up all over again.	I might have true satisfaction—a job that matters to me and enhances my life.
I'll have to acquire new skills.	I'll rediscover the energy and drive that I've lost in my current job.
Such a big change is scary and destabilizing for me and my family.	I'm older and wiser. My experience will help me manage even a very different job.

thing to you. If you don't love it, use it, wear it, or have room for it, get rid of it. The same is true for a job—if you don't like it, do it well, and profit from it financially and/or intellectually, then you have to leave. But let's take some more time to think it through. The best way to contemplate a change is to look at the pros and cons. I'll get you started.

Prepare for a change

Research options. Before you make any move, take the time to study the career or careers that you think might be of interest to you. Cast a wide net—you never know what might appeal to you or where an opportunity might open up. Start online—it's easiest—but as soon as you've narrowed down your options, work your network to try to talk to every person you possibly can in your industry of choice. Best to bring your dream job down to reality before you make any sacrifices to achieve it.

Take a calculated risk. If you're leaving behind a job or career that supports you, and a family if you have one, then it's important to plan very carefully. While you're finding your footing, how will you get by? If you have a partner, can he or she cover you for this period? What sacrifices will you have to make? Maybe you want to go back to school for a higher degree. You'll not only lose income, but you'll acquire debt. Will your new career ever pay back that debt? How long will it take? It's time to do some math, seek some wise advice, and weigh your options.

Acquire skills. If you're looking for work in a competitive new industry, it can help to demonstrate your interest and commitment. What skills do you need but lack? Can you take a class that prepares you? Should you go back to school? Is there an internship or other volunteer work you can do in this area? Taking action to learn more will give you more confidence and make your résumé or application stand out.

Network. Unless your dream "job" is becoming a hermit or painting landscapes alone in the wilderness, you'll be hired by a person. The best way to meet that person is by networking. Your friends and contacts are usually like-minded and, to some extent, share your interests. It's very likely that one of them knows your future employer, directly or indirectly. Now is the time to call in all favors.

Job hunting

You can read whole books describing how to prepare a résumé or what to wear to a job interview. What I want to make sure of is that you clear the clutter around job hunting. Approach the task in a logical, simple way instead of weighing yourself down with too many options and doubts. Be methodical.

Job hunt checklist

1. *Research your options.* Designate a reasonable amount of time you're willing to spend exploring new avenues or potential openings.

2. *Make a list of trusted contacts in your industry of choice.* If you don't have contacts, talk with friends, use their contacts, or search online. Set up informal meetings to discuss your career path. Be open to ideas, but make sure you aren't all over the place: If you play your cards right, this person might be the one who ends up hiring you. Use these contacts to generate new contacts.

3. *Get educated.* If you're changing careers or striving for a promotion, get any training or additional experience you can by taking classes or volunteering.

4. *Make the most of your interview.* Research the position; over-dress—it never hurts; show your enthusiasm for it; highlight your relevant skills. Remember that the interview is just another form

of negotiation. Keep it unemotional (don't mention that you ha\
your old boss), stay on topic, and be clear and straightforward.

5. *Take notes.* Keep a notebook with a page for each intervie\
you have. This will help with your thank-you note and, if you'r\
lucky enough to get an offer, will help you remember all the details of the company and position. It will also come in handy next\
time you initiate a job search.

6. *Follow up.* Ask for a business card at every meeting. Send a
well-thought-out thank-you card or e-mail, reasserting why you
think you're good for the job, hitting any points you may have
missed, and asking for other leads if they might have any. If in
the interview, you connected with the person about a specific topic
or interest, be sure to incorporate that.

Live in the present

No matter how much you hope for a new job, this is the job you
have. Stay focused and be where you are. Don't count on things
changing without your taking action. You design your career. Nobody else thinks about it every day. Are you learning? Growing?
Feeling stimulated? Do you enjoy doing the same thing every day
or do you long for change? It's never too late.

Create an inspiring space

Yes, I'm the guy who just told you to get rid of all the desk toys.
But, really, you can't seriously tell me they actually inspire you to
work. I'm talking about a much higher level of inspiration. Needless to say, your space should be organized and neat. Everything
has a place. It should be well lit. If you're stuck in a cubicle with
overly bright fluorescent lighting that shines directly down on
your head, I suggest leaving it off (or asking someone to unscrew
the bulb above your cube) and bringing in inexpensive desk or

floor lamps. Your workspace should be reasonably quiet. Classical music often helps people work. (If you're in a cubicle, of course use headphones or play music so quietly that it can't be heard from the next cube over.) While your workspace should not be overwhelmed with personal objects or gimmicky toys, it should be a place where you enjoy working, a place that promotes calm and focus, and aids your concentration and efficiency.

Make it pleasant. You see it every day, but don't overdo it. You don't want your office or desk so personalized that it looks like you've been there forever and will be there until the end of time. You're building a career, remember? You expect to be promoted or to move onward and upward.

Build strong professional relationships

Every career requires good personal relations. Even if you're typing at a computer all day or talking on the phone, you want the people at the other end of the line to see you as a person. Your connections will help you land new jobs. Your negotiations will guarantee your success in those jobs. The boundaries you set will keep those relationships healthy and respectful.

Make connections

I don't believe in schmoozing if schmoozing involves being a fake. But you should by all means find people to connect with in your field and cultivate relationships with them. The main reason for doing this is simple: humans are social beings. You'll be happier in your job if you have colleagues you count as friends. Plus, when it's time to look for your next gig, it can't hurt to be plugged into a network of people in your industry you can trust.

Master negotiations

In almost every job there is constant negotiation. You negotiate with your coworker for the more desirable shift. You negotiate with a salesman for a price. You negotiate with your boss for a raise. You negotiate with a client to agree on a plan. There are two important things to keep in mind when you negotiate. The first is to check your emotions at the door. Emotions at the negotiation table are the worst kind of clutter. They will distract you, trip you up, and impede your best decisions. This is business. The person with whom you're negotiating is trying to get the best deal possible, just like you are. Don't be manipulative in a negotiation. It can only backfire. Make your case as best you can without taking it personally if things don't go your way. The second thing to remember is that a negotiation is not a fight. Don't try to win. Winning isn't the goal. The goal is to come to an agreement where each party feels satisfied with the exchange. If you aren't willing to compromise, you're likely to end up with nothing to show for your efforts. Very few negotiations are life and death, so keep a sense of perspective and your sense of humor.

Establish and respect boundaries

You might end up making great friendships through your work. Just be conscious of the boundaries you set and when you risk crossing them. Indiscretions are a lot like clutter. A misspoken word may be innocent enough, but too many words in the wrong place can be a lot like that stuff you hate clogging your garage. If you share intimacies with a work friend over drinks, make sure it's someone you trust. You might want to be clear that conversations that happen outside the office stay outside the office. If you show up late to work because you spent the night with a new boyfriend, don't spend all day on the phone reporting the details to your friends so loudly that all your coworkers can hear. Make it a rule to never forward work e-mails with snarky comments about the sender—you'd be amazed how easy it is to hit reply all. And, always, always, think hard before sending personal e-mails on company computers. When you use work facilities, what you send is open to scrutiny by your employer. If you'd regret someone reading a specific e-mail, don't send it in the first place.

Be flexible and curious

It's easy to get caught in a rut. You know your job, you do it well. Then some too-young new manager comes along and expects you to say "how high?" when he says "jump!" Remember that you will show your best self if you are open to change, hungry to acquire new skills, willing to work in a team, and eager to share information.

Manage stress

Stress—that catch-all word that encompasses all the anxiety, anger, fear, and pent-up tension that clutters your emotions and makes it hard to relax. Stress doesn't just take an emotional toll on your body—it damages your health, your productivity, your sense of self, and maybe even your wallet as you seek relief through retail therapy. It even affects your diet as you wolf down lunch at your desk, eat a candy bar to make it over the hump of the day, or reward your hard work with comfort food. There are hundreds of options for how to manage stress. One person I know was so sick from the stress of her job that her doctor told her the only solution was to quit. She thought he was crazy, but when she did take another job, a chronic, debilitating health problem faded into a manageable one. You can improve your blood pressure and/or cholesterol by making changes in how you approach your job stress—particularly if you eat to make yourself feel better. I'll talk more about how to relieve stress in the Health chapter.

Face fears

Fear is paralyzing. You fear your boss, so you don't stand up for yourself. You fear failure, so you don't invest time and energy in new ideas. You fear the unknown, so you stay in a job that isn't right for you. You fear seeming like a jerk, so you don't tell your employees what to do. Fear and clutter are very similar. Both paralyze you and keep you from making your best decisions. Just as clutter can overtake your home, so can fear overtake your mind. It keeps you stuck in a life that isn't your ideal. Work hard, think clearly, and set goals that make sense for your life. Face the fears that stand in the way of those goals.

Confronting your boss

Your boss has power over you. There's no getting around it. A higher position means greater responsibility and a bigger salary, and in all likelihood your boss has more experience than you do under her belt. But just because your boss has the power to fire you doesn't mean that your interactions should be overshadowed by that dynamic. Treat your boss with the respect she is due, and expect respect in return.

Don't be shy about asking for a raise and/or a promotion if you feel that the work you've done deserves to be rewarded. Make your case in a clear-cut, practical way. The best way to secure a raise is to overperform. If you do the minimum required, you earn the minimum pay. By working as if you hold a higher position, you earn that position. After at least a year of stellar work, it is appropriate to ask for a raise. Don't surprise your boss by demanding a raise when he's heading to the restroom between meetings. Instead, if he isn't in the habit of conducting performance reviews, request a meeting and let him know that you'd like to discuss opportunities for growth. Set a positive tone in the meeting. Describe your performance, stick to the facts, show that you have exceeded expectations, state your case clearly and succinctly, give examples to support your reasoning, and explain your near-term career goals.

Take the same straightforward approach whether you're addressing problems with your workload, dealing with a miscommunication, or hoping for a change in your responsibilities. Don't clutter the discussion by bringing up multiple issues at once. Just present your issue, suggest a fair solution, and stay open to alternate solutions. Finally, be sure to give your boss time to think things over. It's hard to respond on the fly. If she doesn't give you an answer, or he gives you an answer that you don't like, simply restate the answer you are hoping to hear and ask if he or she can think about it for a day or a week—depending on how much more money you want!

Managing employees

Think about it—when you set clear expectations by stating what you expect in a concise, uncluttered way, everyone thrives. Do the people who work for you come into work every day knowing exactly what is expected of them? Do their jobs match their skills? Are they given opportunities to learn and grow? Are you respectful of their personal space and personal lives? When issues come up, do you remain cool-headed and respond professionally, without letting your emotions get the better of you?

As with so many other things—your house, your desk, your relationships—you can't clean up something once and expect it to stay that way forever. The same is true when it comes to managing employees. In addition to regular performance reviews, you should regularly take the time to check in. Do they feel clear on what they're supposed to get done every day? Are you giving them the tools to do it? Keep channels of communication open. Admit your own mistakes and allow your employees to be human, too.

As a manager, it is your right and privilege to make changes that will improve the way business is done. Don't be afraid to establish firm policies with your employees. Don't worry about what they think of you. You're not here to win a popularity contest, though you should certainly try to establish a comfortable, pleasant working environment.

Before you make changes, bring your issues to your employees. Listen to their suggestions with an open mind. If a situation is complicated and personal, allow anonymous recommendations or talk one-on-one.

Changing jobs

As I mentioned, there are plenty of good reasons to change jobs. Don't be afraid to do so when the time is right. When people hoard stuff they don't need, I tell them, "If you don't love it, get rid of it." You only have one life. If your job is weighing you down, if you're burned-out, uninspired, or see no hope of advancement, then it's time to make your move.

Getting fired

It happens to the best of us. No matter how much you hate your boss or your job, getting fired is shocking and hurtful. If you love your job and respect your boss, it's even worse. But once you've gotten over the initial shock, the best thing you can do for yourself is rebound as quickly as possible. Do your best to objectively understand why they let you go. Do you lack skills that you thought you possessed? Was it a personal conflict? Were you visibly unhappy or underperforming? If you have an exit interview, take the opportunity to ask for feedback and to thank your boss for the experience. It may feel embarrassing or painful, but it will earn you respect (and a possible recommendation in the future). Don't burn bridges, not with your boss and not with other colleagues. No bad-mouthing. It's unprofessional, and it won't help you get your next job.

Once you've had time to absorb the news, look for the silver lining. What opportunities does this unexpected crossroads present? Can you land a different or better job? Is it time to pursue a new direction? What changes would you like to make in your skills, your career, and your performance?

Saying good-bye
No matter how much you loved your job, there's always a sense of relief when you leave. You never have to deal with that annoying client on the phone. All the unresolved problems get handed over to the new "you." You're *outta there*. That's all fine and good, but again: don't burn bridges. Respect everyone and leave on good terms. Rise above pettiness. Be gracious. If you leave behind a messy trail of disorganized, unfinished work, your reputation will be soiled. As soon as you know you're leaving, start organizing your work for a clean handoff.

- Remove all your personal belongings and purge personal files or e-mails from your computer.
- Prepare a status report summarizing all your current projects. Include files and contact information where relevant.
- Notify your contacts that you'll be leaving. Tell them the date of your last day and give them the name of the person whom they should contact once you're gone.

- If appropriate, send an e-mail announcing your new position and contact information to all relevant contacts.
- If acceptable to your current employer, leave with digital files containing all the e-mails and other contact information you might need in the future.
- Depart on good terms. Say good-bye to your colleagues. Thank the people who added something to your experience. If there's a dull office party in your honor, smile and eat the cake.

Celebrate successes

Building a career is hard, and sometimes you work so hard that you forget to celebrate the progress you make. When you get a new job, it's tempting to (as the cliché goes) hit the ground running, but I encourage you to do everything you can to take a vacation between jobs. Make it part of your negotiations. Take as long a vacation as you can afford. Being between jobs is one of the most liberated times you have: you've said good-bye to all the responsibilities of your old job and you have the security of knowing a new job is waiting for you. This is the best time to enjoy time off, free from the weight of any job responsibilities. Your cell phone won't ring. You shouldn't have to check e-mail. Work to get your headspace organized and think about your priorities and plans for the coming year. Make the most of it.

Also mark the successes that don't involve changing jobs. A client heaps praise on your work. You land a new account. Or less tangible moments: You finally talk to your boss about the problems you've been having getting your work done. We live in a culture where it's common to complain about work, but it's important to acknowledge the good things in life. You work hard. Share your successes, small and big, with friends and loved ones. Go out to dinner or treat yourself to a massage. Life is short.

And then there's the stuff . . .

When I declutter homes, one of the words that comes up a lot is "space." Open space is an important element to feeling relaxed and comfortable in your home. When it comes to organizing a workspace, relaxation and comfort aren't the primary goals. Work is about efficiency and productivity. You need to know where things are. You need to get things done in order of priority. The more neat and logically organized your workspace is, the better you will be at your job. Look around your office (or wherever you work). Is it the space of someone you would hire, trust, and promote if you owned the business? Now look at the space of someone whose work or position you admire. How do the spaces compare?

You did a Quick Purge of the physical clutter in your office. Now it's time to really clear it out. Take a good, hard look at your space and be honest with yourself. Do you need that presentation from five years ago or the files you inherited on the project that got scrapped? How many shoes are under your desk? How many shopping bags are in your desk drawer? When you look for a pen, do you have to dig under piles of salt and pepper packets? You'll never clean up your career if you don't have a clutter-free environment in which to thrive. Again, the clutter-clearing process I use is consistent across emotional and physical clutter:

- Create a vision for your career. Every item in your workspace should contribute to that vision. (See why I don't like the desk toys?)
- Overcome obstacles. Papers accumulate like nothing else. The sheer volume of files can be daunting, but don't let the size of the task intimidate you. Just start with one area of your office or desk and work in steps. You can do this.

- Commit time, even if it's only purging one pile every day.
- Lunchtime is a good time to purge. Let your colleagues know what you are doing and ask for help, you might even inspire them to clean up, too.
- Set boundaries. Your desk is for working—that means you need space on it to do so. Papers belong in files, where they can be found when needed. Files belong in file cabinets. Keep your computer desktop clean and your e-mail inbox under control.
- Make changes to your work routines in order to manage the clutter in your workspace on an ongoing basis.
- Live in the present. This is the job you have now. Don't allow yourself to work in an unpleasant space because you hope it will change one day.
- Face fears. Decluttering your office may mean facing issues you never dealt with. Is your hatred for your job buried under a ten-foot-tall to-file pile? Are you using office clutter to bury your dreams? Use what you learn to make changes. This new space and clarity will help you define your vision.
- Celebrate successes. A clean workspace is a great foundation for a thriving career. Use the energy it brings you to take you even further.

3

Family

Learning to juggle

I hadn't heard from my former client Julie for several years, during which time she gave birth to two babies, a girl and a boy. Then, out of the blue, she wrote me, saying, "I think you'd be proud of me, Peter. Amos and I seem to be adapting to this major life change. Yes, we've lost some of our time together as a couple, but we balance nights out with enjoying time together with the kids (instead of just handing them off to the other parent as if they are chores instead of people). We're teaching the little ones to respect other people's time and space. We have standards in our house, but the babies are reminding us that it's okay to play, to mess things up, and to break from routines when it makes sense. I know it doesn't sound like 'cleaning up house,' but the process feels the same to me. Our lives are busy, but uncluttered."

The greater the number of people who live in your home, the more you have of everything. More possessions to store, more opinions to accommodate, more mouths to feed, and more conflicts to navigate. With you, your partner, and—if it's in the cards—some kids, the sheer volume of necessary stuff can be enough, and then all the extra "clutter" can become quickly overwhelming. The competing schedules, the daily worries and concerns, the demands that pull you in different directions. The kids' tantrums. The everyday grind. This is the endless clutter of family life.

Dear Peter:
Asking what really is important in life helped so much! For me, it was hard to see how messy my daughter's bedroom was, so full of piles of toys, papers and books she resisted giving away. It really was too much. I was very stressed about it.

After reading your book, I understood it was possible to tackle the problem without an argument. For the first time, I talked peacefully with my teenage daughter about the clutter in her bedroom and helped her, step by step, to examine each part of the room and to make her own decisions about what to keep, give, or toss with no pressure. We used the Kick Start and it worked wonders. As we went through her stuff, during two weekends, she got motivated and did a really good job. Now she is so proud of herself and I am, too. And, best of all, she stopped sneezing since her organized space can be cleaned more often and is now free of dust!

With so much going on, it's easy to lose track of what's important. Every day is full of tough decisions: Are you going to wait for your daughter to finish making a Valentine for her daddy—even if it means she'll be late to school? Do you stay at work to finish a project or hurry to make it home before the kids' bedtime?

How much time do you need for yourself—or should you sacrifice that until the children are older? Making sure your children are healthy, safe, educated, and happy is challenge enough. But you're also in charge of presenting the world to them. How does it all work? Is it fair? What are they entitled to? What must they earn? What can they give back? How should they treat other people? What ideas, dreams, habits, and beliefs will they form? If you don't honor and respect your space and the things you own, your relationship with what you have and where you live will quickly sour. The same is true for people. If you don't honor and respect your family, those relationships will sour, too.

You are a central figure in your children's lives. You and your partner (if you have one) are setting the tone for the family. Don't let a chaotic home and an impossibly full schedule get in the way of finding happiness and balance for your family. At the same time, in all the hubbub of family life, it's easy to lose track of yourself. Is your family so cluttered that the individual relationships are being lost? Are there unresolved conflicts and missed opportunities for joy? Is there a sense of imbalance and chaos that overshadows the spirit of your home?

Dear Peter:
Clutter is stealing from my family . . . literally! It is stealing our time and energy. I have two boys, and we have excess everything.

My six-year-old comes home with enough paper to kill several trees each school year. He is picking up on our bad habits by never wanting to throw away or get rid of anything. As I work with him on this, I know I'm telling him, "Do what I say, not what I do."

We have toys and clothes for both of our kids—age sixteen months and six years—and every stage between. I find myself saving clothes for the younger one that the older one never wore because "I might use it next time." I never do.

Quiz
How Cluttered Is Your Family?

1. Which sentence best describes your experience of becoming a parent?
    a. *I'm constantly juggling all my responsibilities, but most of the balls seem to stay in the air.*
    b. *I love my children, but I've lost touch with who I used to be.*
    c. *Being a parent seems like a natural extension of who I am.*

2. How would you describe the world that your children experience?
    a. *It's a seat-of-the-pants operation, but we have fun.*
    b. *They're often overloaded with options and activities.*
    c. *They have fun and feel secure in their familiar routines.*

3. When I am trying to get us out the door and my children are too slow:
    a. *I let them take their time. Being late isn't the end of the world.*

    b. I pick them up and put them in the car, shoes or no shoes.

    c. I try to be creative, inventing a game or a race to speed things up.

4. When my child does something she knows is wrong:
    a. She gets a time out so she can think about what she did.
    b. She is punished. End of story.
    c. We always talk it through. I try to understand what's behind her actions.

5. There are things I wish I had time for:
    a. And I try, but I just can't squeeze everything in.
    b. But they'll have to wait till the kids leave the house.
    c. And I find a way to do enough to keep me sane.

6. The working parent(s) in your house:
    a. Is a little out of touch with the routines and rules, but we do our best to communicate.
    b. Breaks all the rules—who wants to discipline kids when there's so little time together?
    c. Works hard to make sure the children get consistent treatment from parents and caregivers alike.

7. In your house, the children's stuff:
    a. Is a constant challenge, but I try to get rid of stuff as they outgrow it.
    b. Has taken over the whole house, including the master bedroom.

    c. Is under control. Everything has a place and always goes back where it belongs at the end of the day.

8. When I spend time with my children:
    a. I'm often juggling food preparation, laundry, etc.
    b. I can't help multitasking—but I'm there if they need me.
    c. I set aside a specific time during the day when they know they have my undivided attention.

9. When it comes to household responsibilities:
    a. I do more than my partner, but he or she might feel the same way!
    b. I carry all the weight. My partner has no idea how hard it is.
    c. We've worked out a balance . . . most of the time.

10. As my children get older and more independent:
    a. I plan to catch up on years of sleep deprivation.
    b. I'll continue to devote myself to caring for them full-time.
    c. I look forward to slowly reclaiming some of the interests or activities I've sacrificed.

How cluttered is your family?

If your answers are mostly As:
Well, nobody said being a parent was easy. Did you know that the word "child" comes from the same root as the word "chaos"? (Actually, I just made that up! It's not true, but it

might as well be.) You're juggling the whole family's diverse needs, activities, and stuff, and you're doing a pretty good job of it. But there's always room for improvement. A calm, clear, and simple world is the best environment for a child. More important than keeping your children busy is giving them the time and space to explore, to be creative and social, and to connect with you. Clutter gets in the way of a smoothly functioning space—it's the same in families. To make things run as smoothly as possible (and who doesn't want that), we need to clear the physical as well as mental and emotional clutter and open some space. In this chapter, I'm going to help you bring a little more order to the chaos. You'll set your priorities and figure out how to live by them.

If your answers are mostly Bs:
You love your children to no end, but it's proving tough for you to strike the right balance. Have you sacrificed all your personal needs, now and in the future, for the sake of your children? Will that make you the best parent you can be? And how do you set priorities when you structure your children's day? Do you rush them or take time to listen to them? Are you setting a foundation of communication that will benefit your relationship with your children for the rest of your life and theirs—or are you too busy multitasking or making sure they get to ballet class or soccer practice? Children need limits and routines. They thrive on them. But the very first step is establishing communication so your child knows what is expected of him. It may be tough to face your flaws as a parent, but doing so, and being open to adjustments, will benefit the whole family.

If your answers are mostly Cs:
I'm impressed. It seems that you take the time to listen to your children, to hear what they have to say, and to respond to them. If that's all you do as a parent, you're already doing a great job. You value your children, see them as people with needs, ideas, thoughts, and opinions—people who deserve your respect. As you read this chapter, watch to see if this philosophy is consistent throughout your parenting, and look to identify areas where you could fine-tune your approach.

Imagine the family life you want

Families of every kind exist now and it's tough—if not impossible—to tailor a one-size-fits-all solution. Although I'm taking a middle road in this chapter by talking in terms of a nuclear family, this approach can be used when clearing the clutter in your relationships with aging parents, siblings, and other extended family. The basic principles are always the same, only the applications may vary a little.

Being part of a family, like being in a relationship, involves balancing other people's needs and desires with your own. The difference in a family is that as parents, you need to take the lead. You need to offer your children a calm, organized world that prepares them for a healthy, happy life. You need to find the balance between guiding your children and teaching them to be independent. You need to model behavior, establish routines, and set limits while still letting kids be kids. It's a tall order, even if you have excellent parental instincts. Both you and your children are getting older. Their needs are changing constantly—school, sports, music, activities, friends—all come in and go out of their (and your) lives so quickly it makes your head spin. It is easy to get caught up in the busy-ness of everyday life and lose focus on the bigger picture. Before you know it, your family life is so cluttered it feels uncentered and out of control. Let's go back to the basic question—our starting point—for a moment:

What is the life I want to live with my family?

I phrase the question this way for a reason. Although we can all strive for an ideal life, you can't change who the people in your family are. No matter how hard you work to create and execute a vision, it will never match your dream of a "perfect" family. The reason for this is simple—there is no such thing as "the perfect family" or "the ideal family." Families are as varied and diverse as you can imagine. There is no one-size-fits-all here. Part of the thrill and terror of creating and raising a family is that no one has done it exactly like you before. We are all pioneers on this frontier, each with new discoveries to be made every day. The best you can do is focus on what you want for yourself and them, open the lines of communication and understanding, clear the path, and work to find a happy balance. Your home must be a haven for you and your family, a place of peace and calm where all of you feel valued and safe. Your home should reflect your values and priorities—for it is in the home that children first learn what is important, what is valued, and how to live their lives. It is also in the home that children learn the value and place of material possessions in their lives—does the family control what it owns or does the stuff rule the home? Are you in control of what you own or are you power-less when facing its onslaught? These are basic yet profound lessons that the child absorbs in the home and carries into the world.

Here are some starting points to help you create a vision for the life you live with your family.

- **Love and joy**

Sure, it should go without saying that creating a home full of love and joy is the goal of family life. But then there are meals to prepare, diapers to change, playdates to arrange, and school projects and extracurriculars, and sometimes two careers and babysitters, and home repairs to be done and bills to pay. . . . You do it all out of love, and with love, but sometimes it's tough for anyone to *experience* the love. In today's busy world, love is something you practically have to put in the calendar.

- **Balance of fun and growth**

Childhood is a time for wonder and imagination. It should be happy and fun. It's a fleeting time, and you want your children to get the most out of it. At the same time, you want your kids to grow into healthy, productive, successful, happy, loving, and loveable members of society. As a parent, you have to balance these goals for your children. Generally, at school, time is strictly divided into fun (recess) and education (classes). But at home (and in some great schools), the distinction is more subtle. You can have fun as a family while encouraging your children's curiosity, guiding them in terms of social and intellectual growth, and helping them find pleasure and satisfaction in expanding their minds.

- **Trust and communication**

A family needs a core of resilience, a strong foundation of trust to sustain you through hard times (adolescence, illness, external problems, family conflict). Trust is the knowledge that your family loves you unconditionally and is always there for you. Because you trust your family, you don't need to talk about unconditional love and other sentimental stuff all the time. You don't need constant confirmation from them. But that trust needs to be bolstered by good communication and an underlying sense of security and

love. You can't always rely on unspoken truths to see you through some of the hardest moments for a family. Sometimes you just need to talk it through.

Good communication, like organization, needs to be part of the family's way of life. Getting a teenager to talk about her thoughts and feelings is a challenge any day of the week. But if that teenager was raised knowing she could express herself freely, without fear of judgment or ridicule, you'll have much better luck keeping the lines of communication open as adolescence casts its shadow over her life (not to take too dark a stance).

• Independence and fulfillment

Every member of the family is an individual, as well as a part of the whole family. As a parent, you have to balance your role as a caregiver with your needs as an individual. If you sacrifice all of your time and energy to your family without finding a way to socialize with adults, to have a romantic life, or to feel intellectually stimulated, to maintain a healthy body and mind, the whole family will suffer. Remember: You're modeling adulthood for your children—don't create a martyr model of parenthood. Being an empty, self-sacrificing shell of a person is hardly the role model you want them to see. Of course, it's tough, if not impossible, to satisfy all of these needs to the fullest every single day. Parenting usually involves some level of self-sacrifice, but you need to strive for a healthy balance that works for you and your family.

Your children are also individuals. They need space to form their own opinions, adopt their own interests, and pursue their own goals. Of course, children need stimulation, but they also benefit from private time and quiet space. You can foster independent thinking by creating a safe, open play space with age-appropriate toys they can explore. There's no need to hover over them, responding to their every sound and motion. I'm not saying you should

Activity
Define Your Vision for Your Family

If you have a partner, try this exercise together. If you and your partner are at odds when it comes to the family, this can be both a tool for defining your vision and increasing your communication. Try doing the exercise separately, then compare your answers. If your children are old enough, they can and should be brought into creating the vision for the family.

Words that describe your current family life:

Words that describe the family life you want to have:

- _____

- _____

- _____

- _____

- _____

- _____

Describe what your ideal family would be like:

Describe what changes you and your family need to make in order to achieve your ideal:

leave your one-year-old unsupervised, but you can allow him to travel into the world of his imagination without interruption in a safe space. (Believe me, you'll appreciate the independence you cultivate since it gives you time to check e-mail or get dinner on the table.) If you allow your children this space from the start, they'll learn how to carve it out for themselves as they get older.

Clear the clutter of unreal expectations

These are starting points, but I want your family to take the time to discuss your shared vision for your life together. Everyone has different and fluctuating expectations.

The media gives us an image of the perfect family. It includes a big house, with a couple of big cars in the garage, a big TV, and a big kitchen where everyone eats big meals. Playing happily in the yard are two or more well-dressed, well-behaved children who

Dear Peter:
My home says family and the pictures on the wall are of happy happy joy, but in reality my life is not perfect. Children grow up and they move on. Control is an illusion. I need to learn to let go of my *Waltons*, *Leave It to Beaver* illusion and face the fact that my script for them was not their script. Life is ebb and flow, not a once-and-for-all "Whew! I did it, now you can all live happily ever after." My home is a sad place, but not an ending place. I can face my disappointments and accept them. The pictures do not mean it wasn't real. There were very good times and there will be again.

not only excel in school, but who also have various talents like violin playing or sports that will one day get them into the colleges of their choice. The parents in the family have successful careers, great bodies, an active sex life, blindingly white teeth, warm relationships with their children, and plenty of "me time" for shopping, massages, and the like. Sounds pretty good, doesn't it?

What this image ignores is the responsibilities that correspond with that suburban dream. Children have to be guided. They need to spend quality time with adults who are attentive to their emotional, intellectual, and physical development. This takes real time and involves more than driving them home from soccer practice, putting food on the table, and getting the laundry folded (though these things still have to get done). You need to build a real, human relationship with your children. I can't say it enough. This responsibility comes with the decision to have kids. Schools are not parents. Caregivers are not parents (though the right caregiver can be an excellent substitute). As a parent you have to deal with the constant struggle to balance time with your children and time to attend your own needs and desires. I can't define the balance for you, but I can recommend that you periodically listen to the song "Cat's in the Cradle." A little melodramatic? Sure. But there's a sobering lesson in there, too. Don't miss out on your children's youth. It's fleeting. Yes, preserve yourself. Your children need you to be a whole person. But make room for real family time.

> Dear Peter:
> I inherited all of my parents belongings from a four-bedroom home when I was twenty-one (a "few" years ago). It has taken me a long time to let go of "things," unconsciously playing the role of caretaker and preserver of my parents' memory. All that "stuff" took up so much of my space and of my life. I've cleared clutter in stages and at last got rid of the obligatory storage unit. During this process, I reinitiated contact with my only sister, from whom I'd been estranged for over thirty years. And something remarkable happened. Our relationship started to rekindle—and last month she flew from San Francisco to Washington, D.C., to visit me—the first time she'd been on the East Coast in over thirty years. Moving these "things" out of my life truly gave me space for me—to see clearly what was important in my life, and to help me have it.

Watch out for obstacles

Children need to play, and playing can and should be loud and messy. How can your daughter pretend to be a tiger if she doesn't roar a huge roar? How can your son figure out what happens when you mix red and blue if he doesn't attempt to pour one pot of paint into the other? Most families have some amount of chaos, and I'm all for it. Don't confuse chaos with clutter. Clutter is the disorganization that gets in the way of everything you want your family to be.

Cluttered priorities

Do you let your kids stay up so late to say good night to a spouse who's working late that they have trouble waking up to go to school? On a shopping expedition, do you buy your son the toy he begs for just to shut him up? Is it really important for your kids to put away their toys when you can do it much faster and you don't want to get in a fight about it at the end of a long day? Running a household is a balancing act between fun and growth. I know it can be hard to impose limits on your kids and establish healthy routines, but limits and routines are important parts of decluttering your family life and maintaining some order (and your sanity!).

Dear Peter:

Since the birth of our daughter six years ago, I find myself feeling guilty for cleaning when she is home and wanting my attention. I have gained sixty pounds and find it hard to justify the time for working out when I should be straightening up and cleaning. It is a constant struggle for me internally. I want to clean and have a nice, peaceful home. I want to exercise. But I also want to spend time with my child.

This year I have vowed to wipe the slate clean and start new. Having a healthy home and a healthy body are my new goals. I just pray every day that I can keep this vow to myself and my family.

The writer of this e-mail doesn't want to clean house or take care of herself because she wants to be with her daughter. But what example is she setting? A better option than stopping everything to attend to her daughter is to involve her daughter in the cleaning, to have fun together, and then to focus on other things, herself included, when her daughter goes to school. Make no mistake! Being with your children is no excuse for letting the world they live in and the parents they love fall apart before their very eyes.

No shared vision

Earlier, I asked you to describe your vision for your family. Did you attempt to do that alone? It's not a useless exercise, but it won't get you far. No one person can set the vision for an entire family. You are a group of individuals with separate personalities and needs and you must agree upon a shared vision that accommodates all of you.

Letting kids self-parent

Even small children have strong opinions about how they want to spend their time and what color they want their rooms to be. Great—let your kids have a say in their playdates and paint colors. But that doesn't mean your child decides what time to go to bed or whether teeth need brushing. You are the parent and you need to be the parent. You know better than your child what is good for him. Working parents often have so little time with their children that they don't want to spend it disciplining them. You don't have to be forceful and strict. You can still be gentle and understanding. But you make the rules and they follow them. Keep it straight.

No boundaries

From the day they are born, children demand your attention during every waking second and many sleeping moments. It isn't hard to spend all your time being a parent: cooking, cleaning, working glue-stick miracles. But much as you shouldn't let a job take over your life, you need to learn how to make your children your priority, but not your sole focus. You need to carve out time for your own friends and interests, and most importantly your partner, because if you don't take care of yourself, you teach your children that you and your needs don't matter. Don't be a martyr. It isn't helping your children form a sense of identity, and it certainly isn't helping you.

No division of labor

Taking care of children and running a house is a full-time job, but in most families today both parents work, so obviously neither should be saddled with all the housewivery. No matter how you divvy up the tasks, you're both bound to feel like you're doing too much (and you probably are). Don't blame the other person. Parenting and housekeeping are endless jobs and you're not going to make it any easier by resenting the other person. However, if you married a man who thinks you should be ironing his socks after working all day, it's time to talk.

Cluttered Communication

Remember those "terrible twos"? Young children say "no" constantly, as if they're programmed to do it. ("Are you ready for your bath?" "No!") You knew that this was how they were forging independence, so instead of caving to their whims (and having a filthy child) or getting into an argument, you tried to make the bath more attractive ("You can play with your blue monster!" "Yes, bath.") As your children get older, they never really stop playing the "no" game, they just get better at it. Your teenager has to roll her eyes at everything you do. Your son has to play his music at ear-splitting volume. But now that they're in that "obnoxious adolescent" phase instead of being chubby-cheeked toddlers, you're less inclined to spice up your demands with blue monsters. Instead, you dig yourselves deeper and deeper into a "because I said so!" argument that can only end with doors slamming and someone getting grounded. You are both so determined to win—and instead you both lose. You need to build a foundation of open communication and respect, ideally one strong enough to weather the teenage years.

Dear Peter:

I can look back upon my childhood and remember my bedroom—filled to the brim with things/stuff/junk. Some I liked, some I loved, and a lot of it, I had no idea what to do with. My father built me shelves, but I soon outgrew those, too. . . . I can recall my mom and dad saying to me, "Go clean your room" and it was so overwhelming to me I wouldn't clean it—I didn't know where to begin. I don't recall my parents giving me permission to throw stuff away or donate things. I found myself as an adult feeling like that CHILD again—I "needed" permission to toss the clutter—I had never learned as a child how to purge/declutter, and I took that idea with me as an adult.

Declutter your family

Our family lives today are more cluttered than ever and everything seems to move faster and faster. In the blur of daily life, it's

Activity
What's Getting in the Way of Having My Ideal Family?

Reviewing the sections above, write down the obstacles that stand between you and the family life you'd like to enjoy.

• _____

• _____

• _____

easy to lose track of who you are and where you want to be. Before you know it, you're going through the motions of being a father or mother, a son or daughter, without feeling like there's any time or space to give or receive the protected warmth, love, and support that a family should provide.

Commit time

You can't snap your fingers and restore order and calm to your family. If you don't know where to begin, it never hurts to start with the stuff.

Reassess your family time

Decluttering your family time while your children are young is your responsibility. Preteen children can't be responsible for balancing activities, chores, and personal time, though it's never too early to start talking about the choices that you are making as you plan your schedule and go about your day.

Dear Peter:

The clutter in my head is a wall between me and my husband that I cannot even begin to discuss with him (I have tried), because it comes down to the actual stuff. We have furniture in the cellar that is just taking up space, but it came from his family so we have to keep it. Every single thing has some sentimental attachment! I resent it and I feel like that past is sucking the life out of my future. I see it sometimes in my children and their inability to let anything go, physical and emotional. In my husband, I see a fear of dying without anyone to know or care who you are. I was raised differently and death doesn't hold the same fear. He worries constantly and doesn't sleep well and doesn't even see that all the stuff is linked to that mind-set. It makes me sad and frantic at the same time. The clutter, I think, is impossible to get rid of for him because it *is* him. We have stuff that he had as a child. He doesn't look at it or play with it, but it represents some sort of safety. I see my house becoming isolated and inhospitable. It is for me the primary source of discord and pain. But he views it as wonderful to have "rescued" all these things, as if not keeping them somehow jeopardizes his existence.

My thoughts go in circles, trying to work within the bounds of not making him hurt by just throwing things away—I have never done that—and trying to resolve or see into the reason that this stuff is so important so that I can

help. But after twenty-three years, seeing how little headway I have made into understanding the issues, is now just as emotionally overwhelming to me as the physical stuff is. . . . Yet I would rather have the emotional discord in my own head than lose him. So I keep pushing aside the emotions that this issue brings out and I blame the feelings of stress and anger on other things in my world, like work or school or whatever. But I know in my heart that the real issue is how our family relates to stuff and the walls those reactions are building between us. All is fine on the surface (and maybe I am the one who needs help), but underneath I feel constantly terrified. It is much easier to just ignore it and try to embrace the chaos.

Rethink your schedule

Willow was accustomed to a busy schedule—her dad, Malcolm, liked to plan lots of classes and activities for them. But when Willow started preschool at age three, things changed. One day, outside music class, she refused to go in. Bursting into tears, she said to Malcolm, "I want to be home, at our house, with just you." No matter how busy your life and your children's lives are, it's important to include "at-home" time. This is downtime that you spend with your children. It is time when the children have your full attention. It is valuable time where you talk and play and build the foundation of the relationship you hope to have with your children for the rest of their lives. Even if you work full-time and find this time hard to carve out, do it. Even if it only happens once a week, make sure it is consistent and that you hold it sacred. Don't overschedule. Keeping children busy isn't the answer to parenting.

Rethink multitasking

Let me say this upfront—I am strongly opposed to multitasking. When it comes to raising kids and building the kind of family you want, your children need your full attention. They don't need it every moment of every day, but they need it frequently and consistently—and when they need it, they need it! They need it when they are upset. They need it when they are talking to you about something important.

Before becoming a stay-at-home mom, Karen had been a successful marketing director for a pharmaceutical company. She was very used to juggling many projects and demands at once and prided herself on this ability. Once her kids came along, she kept a laptop on the kitchen counter and checked e-mails constantly throughout the day. Interestingly, after a family vacation without access to e-mail, she completely changed her approach. "I realized," she told me, "that I was never really giving my kids my full attention and it wasn't good for them or for me." Now the laptop stays on the desk in the home office and e-mail is checked a few times a day. When she is interacting with her children, they get her full attention. When she is responding to e-mails, they get her full attention. Any task she tackles gets her full and focused attention.

To be sure, multitasking is a skill in which parents can take pride. Multitasking gets dinner on the table. But don't let the task at hand steal your attention so that you're uttering mindless "uh-huhs" as your child tells you what happened at the playground. Make eye contact and listen when you talk to your child or you'll pay the price when she won't look up from a video game to tell you how her day was.

Divide and conquer . . . sometimes

Divide parenting responsibilities with your partner or spouse to create and preserve personal time, but maximizing efficiency isn't the be-all and end-all. Don't forget to be a family. Spend time together doing activities that all of you enjoy—being outdoors, visiting friends, going to museums, eating in restaurants. If you take short, manageable outings with your children from a young age, you not only encourage them to develop tastes similar to yours, but you rear children who are comfortable and civilized in the places you frequent.

Ditch the TV

The average American adult spends about three months a year watching TV. Three months! Right there is a major problem. If your family life doesn't meet your ideal vision, stop watching TV for a month. All of you. Think back to what you want for your family. How is your family being nourished? If their diet consists of an overdose of bad reruns and watching the tube just because that's the easiest thing to do, then it's time for a reassessment of what's happening in your home. TV saps time and dulls the brain like nothing else. It turns you and your children into zombies. Instead of zoning out in front of mindless reality shows, have dinner at the dining room table. Talk to one another. Do something crazy together—turn off all the lights in the house and play hide-and-seek in the dark with flashlights. Go bowling. Look at the stars. Build a rocket ship in the back yard—you get the idea! If you're looking for time to connect, unplugging the TV is the easiest first step.

It's never too late to sleeptrain

Sleep is important for growing children and tired adults. If your family's sleep is disrupted on a regular basis—be it by children or grown-ups or street noise—don't just accept being sleep-deprived as your lot in life. Charts and children vary, but the National Sleep Foundation recommends eleven to thirteen hours of sleep for preschoolers; ten to eleven hours for schoolchildren up to age twelve; eight and a half to a little more than nine hours for teens, and adults need seven to nine hours a night. Lack of sleep affects your mood, your judgment, and your general outlook on life. It diminishes your physical health, affecting hormone levels and the immune system. Lack of sleep is also associated with obesity and diabetes. Basically, lack of sleep can very quickly turn you into a crazy person! Take steps toward fixing the problem. It all comes down to respecting yourself, your body, and your family. Invest time in order to cultivate quality time together.

Communicate

Can you and your children discuss and agree on a vision for the family? You can if you've taught your children how to communicate. As they grow, children learn words. They want the ball, they say "ball," they get the ball. This is encouraging, so they expand their vocabularies and start to use more words in more complex ways. If a young child doesn't get what he wants, he cries. But if he is encouraged, over time he'll learn to use words to express his desires and emotions. As your child grows older, his desires and emotions are more and more complex. It continues to be your job to encourage him to express himself and to listen to others. You ask him a question, listen to his response, probe deeper . . .

It is easy to make the rules and expect your children to follow them. This works well to create order in a household, but it doesn't empower your child. It doesn't show her that her ideas have value, that she is a voice who is heard by the family. Remember that if you make all the rules, then your job is to enforce them.

And trust me, you'll spend a lot of time doing it. How much fun is that?

If your child is a valued participant in deciding the rules of the house, then she'll understand why certain behavior is expected and will be more likely to take an active role in planning and enjoying family activities. Instead of focusing on getting only her own needs met, she'll be invested in what works best for the whole family. Engage, support, and communicate with your children, and you will reap the benefits for a lifetime.

When your child is old enough, start to involve him in family decisions. How would he like to spend Saturday? A vacation? Does he prefer his space to be cluttered or organized? Why? What is important to him? What things do we no longer need or use? What should be discarded? How do things make him feel? What choices lie ahead? Teach him to verbalize what's important and to make choices based on priorities. Teach him to make decisions with an uncluttered mind. Your children's contributions to the family vision will evolve as they grow older.

If you have older children, it's never too late to involve them. They will be resistant at first, but if you truly listen and take what they say seriously, you'll start to get real answers out of them.

Set boundaries

You only have so many hours in the day. You can devote all of your waking hours to parenting, but if you lose track of yourself, your marriage, and any outside work you choose to do, you're asking for a midlife crisis. How can you achieve the balance of family life and personal life that you outlined in your vision?

Don't be a martyr. No matter how much you love them, you are not entirely defined by your family. It's easy to lose track of who you are and how you used to spend your time before you had a family. Here are some examples of how you can clear space in your life to make room for a sense of self.

Preserve the master bedroom

The master bedroom is the most important room in the house. It drives your household and sets the tone for everything that takes place in your home. It is the center of your romantic relationship and the place where you are most intimate with your partner. Preserve it as the adult sanctuary it should be. A master bedroom overrun with children's laundry, videos, and toys means you are sacrificing your relationship not for your *children*, but for their *stuff*. Kids' toys are a little like junk mail—glance away for a second and they'll take over the entire house! Make your bedroom a toy-free zone. Even if toys creep in during the day, clear them out—with your children's help—before they go to bed. This will remind everyone that Mom and Dad (or Moms or Dads) are entitled to a private, grown-up life. Your children will not feel excluded from your love. Rather, they will feel grounded by the model of a relationship that their parents take seriously. A cluttered master bedroom is always a huge warning sign in any home that I tackle. Make it your own. Treasure it and guard it well.

Reclaim the bathroom

As parents, you often squeeze in personal hygiene and grooming wherever you can. A toddler watches with fascination as you use the toilet or plays in the bathroom while you shower. That's all fine and good when your kids are little but at some point it has to stop. If multiple family members share one bathroom, lay down clear rules that enable preteens, teenagers, and adults to have privacy and to respect one another's needs and toiletries. Whenever and as soon as you can manage, bring privacy (not secrecy, just privacy) back to the bathroom.

Restore yourself

I am not a big fan of the term "me time." It sounds at once guilty and self-absorbed, as if you know you don't really need the time, but you're taking it anyway. And it suggests that you're doing something frivolous instead of a very necessary mental and physical recharging. So let's call it "personal time." Personal time takes many forms. You might spend it getting a pedicure or running on a treadmill or reading in a cafe. However, if you spend all your personal time shopping, you need to find a new outlet. Shopping only leads to more problems. And don't try to tell me that you find household chores restorative. I want you to take real time—every day if possible—to truly unwind. However you spend the time, do so with the knowledge that this is time you need to be alone in your head, to clear your mind, shake a little of that mental clutter loose and restore yourself mentally and physically. Your whole family will reap the benefits of a balanced, energized, happier you.

Respect yourself

Last Christmas a friend of mine was complaining about her weight. She said she felt like a cow in a bathing suit. Her preteen daughter chimed in with, "Well, you *are* a cow." My friend shrugged it off, but I was horrified. I turned to the girl, with whom I have a friendly rapport, and said, "How rude! I would never speak to my mother that way." My friend said she was used to that behavior in a "preteens-will-be-preteens" way, but I found it unacceptable for two reasons. The first is that you shouldn't let your children treat you worse than you want them to treat others. No interrupting, no insulting, no eye rolling. Second, I worried about the toll such treatment was taking on my friend. How could she feel like a strong, attractive wife and mother if this kind of talk was okay in her home? This kind of throwaway line isn't all that different from the clutter that slowly builds, fills, and eventually chokes the life out of a space. It's not about the single comment (or purchase) so much—though that's bad enough—it's about the cumulative effect of such behavior if it's left unchecked. Children love to see how far they can go. Friendly joking is one thing, but accepting hurtful and demeaning barbs as normal is quite another.

If your children treat you inappropriately, the first step is to make sure that you and the other authority figures in their lives are modeling the right behavior. If your partner is dismissive or condescending to you, you can be sure that your children will follow suit. The next step is to make sure your children understand what is expected of them. Don't just criticize and call attention to bad behavior ("Don't speak that way to your mother!"). Describe simply and clearly the behavior you want to see ("I want you to be nice to me. It makes me feel happy and proud of you. I'm nice to you. People should be kind to each other. That's what I expect from you."). Praise good behavior when you receive it. Kids respond well to positive reinforcement instead of criticism and punishment.

Establish limits and routines

Children thrive when they know what is expected of them. I've seen this over and over again when I declutter homes. Children who cling to old toys and artwork, resist change, and refuse to help clean up come to life when they are involved in the verbalization of goals and given specific tasks that they know are within reach. "Clean this room" falls on deaf ears; "Please fill this crate with toys that you want to give to needy children" inspires immediate action.

Your child's life shouldn't be governed by rules upon rules

upon rules, but if you establish reasonable guidelines for behavior, they will understand and follow. If you're looking for change, consider how you speak to your kids and how you seek to engage them in an activity. Try thinking in terms of involving your child rather than in terms of just getting a task done. This simple change of mind-set can reap rewards—and work wonders!

Model the behavior you expect

Modeling is enormously important. Most of us grew up being told "Do as I say, not as I do," or "Why? Because I said so." But think about what you are actually saying to your child when you use these phrases or when you say one thing but do another. With the first, you are saying that you don't adhere to your own rules. You're admitting a double standard. Do you really expect your kids to respect you and listen to you when you don't listen to yourself? "Because I said so" is just plain lazy. What you're really saying is, "I don't have a good reason," or "I don't think it's worth explaining the reason to you," or "You're too young to understand." Give your children a chance. Even if they don't understand at first, just the knowledge that you're trying to explain reminds them that you see them as thinking human beings capable of making wise decisions. But all this falls under the larger category of modeling the behavior you wish to see in your children. You want them to communicate, you want them to make smart choices, you want them to grow into independent thinkers who are caring, responsible, curious and, yes, civilized!

In dealing with clutter in homes, it's very common for parents to say to me, "You have to get my teenager to clean up and organize his room." I love that challenge—but here's the kicker that most parents hate. The first step in decluttering the teenager's room is to look at the closet in the master bedroom and the current condition of the garage. Parents usually cry foul, but I

don't think this is unreasonable. You can't seriously be annoyed at your child's poor skills when you have few in that area yourself and are modeling exactly the behavior you don't want.

Kids learn most from what they see, not from what they hear. Be loving, and they will be loving. Read books, and they will love reading. Eat healthy food, and they will eat healthy food. Maintain a healthy relationship with your stuff. Value organization. Explain why you want them to do things and they will understand. But raise your voice—and they will raise their voices. Live a cluttered life, and they will live cluttered lives. Model well the behavior you want most from your children.

Follow through

If you don't keep promises or threaten punishments that never come, what kind of response do you expect? When a punishment is threatened but never carried through, your child learns that any behavior is acceptable and acts accordingly. It is equally important to keep your promises to your child—if you said you would do something, do it. Kids have to learn to take you at your word and that they can trust you. Don't threaten taking away the family trip to Disneyland unless you're willing to cancel. Don't promise to spend time with your child, but then take a phone call. Be consistent and your children will feel like the world is a secure and reasonable place (and maybe one day they'll help make it so).

Clean up

Children need to learn from an early age—and see modeled behavior from day one—that you own your stuff and not that your stuff owns you. I can't stress enough the importance of this lesson. Children who grow up in a cluttered home are left with the impression that they are powerless in the face of what they own. Living with clutter sends the implicit message that you are not in

control, that your stuff rules, and you cannot effect change on the world around you. This message can have incredibly negative effects on how children view the world and the kind of adults they become. Effectively, you are teaching helplessness.

There is another problem with cluttered homes. You run the risk of raising children whose primary relationship is with their stuff. These kids can easily develop into spoiled individuals with a sense of entitlement that is repulsive. And I am not just talking about mess. I am talking about having too much—too many TVs, too many books, clothes, toys, video games, gadgets—and being overwhelmed by an irrational need to have more because, in their minds, more is better.

Sometimes children from cluttered homes respond by becoming controlling neat freaks who are terrified of repeating the mistakes their parents made. Either way, kids surrounded by clutter frequently grow into adults with a skewed relationship—with their stuff and with the world around them.

It's never too early or too late for kids to start cleaning up after themselves. It's one of the best, most simple life lessons a child can learn: You make a mess, you clean it up. If your child is young, keep your standards low. If your child puts away one block for every ten you throw in the bin, great. He's being helpful and contributing to the family. Look for ways to make clean-up fun and satisfying—have races, count pieces, make the exercise challenging and even exciting. Model appreciation of a clean room—show how good it makes you feel to go to sleep and wake up to a clean home. One message to learn early is that everything has a place—if there is no more room for another stuffed animal, don't buy any more stuffed animals. And if you can't do that, get rid of one toy to make room for the new one.

If your child is older, it can be very hard to change messy habits. Now is a good time to implement the communication skills you've been working on. Have an honest talk about how the mess makes you feel and ask your child how it makes him feel. If he's perfectly happy with a messy room (and many children are), then I think it's acceptable for him to keep it that way—so long as the mess doesn't cause real problems, like attracting bugs or affecting schoolwork. But a messy common space is a different story. If your child's mess overflows into shared areas, you must talk it through until you reach a solution with which the whole family is comfortable. By the way, this same principle applies to Mom's crafting supplies and Dad's DVD collection. The stuff has to take second place to the growth and health of your family. The things you own and the things you surround yourself with exist to create the vision you have for yourself and your family. If they don't, what are they doing in your home?

Eat real food

Almost every family has a child who is a picky eater at some point in his or her life. Respect your child's pickiness. They usually don't do it to be difficult. Food simply tastes different when you're a child. Developing a taste for a new food or texture can take time. Don't give up after one try. What I don't like to see is parents feeding their children unhealthy foods because it's all they like to eat. Isn't giving her fast food or sweets worse than giving her nothing at all? It won't solve the problem and won't provide the nutrients she needs. I know, you want your child to eat *something*, but that doesn't mean you have to cook six different meals. Learn to make a few healthy, easy-to-prepare meals for the whole family. It might take a few tries, but cooking one meal for the whole family and eating it together (not in front of the TV) will help your child focus on the food and try new things. You'll be surprised how quickly she'll find something she likes. It doesn't matter if she eats the same foods for every meal for a while (check with your pediatrician, of course). When it comes to snacking (and aren't kids always hungry?), kids eat what's readily available—the question is, what are you making available? If you have candy, cookies, chips, and soda, that is what your child will eat. If you have fruit (which actually tastes sweeter than cookies), cheese, whole-wheat crackers, and other wholesome choices, then that is what they will eat. Just keep simple, healthy choices in your home and she'll have no choice but to expand her tastes and learn to eat new foods that are good for her. And remember, cluttered kitchens encourage the easy choice, not the good choice, and no family can be making their healthiest decisions in a cluttered, messy, disorganized space.

Act your age (for better or worse)
Children should act their age. This is a responsibility and a privilege. Let your child know what is expected of him, but don't expect your five-year-old to sit quietly through a dinner party. She is not an adult and shouldn't be forced to act like one.

Give your child fair warning. Before you enter a new circumstance—a store, a birthday party, an adult gathering, a school, a doctor's office, a grocery store—talk to your child about what behavior is expected and why it is important. Make sure your instructions don't translate as, "Whatever you do, don't be yourself and don't have fun." Draw him into the task ("We're trying to get groceries fast, so you can go to the party on time. Can you help me be *fast?*") so he can take pride in his efforts and feel a sense of achievement when you emerge triumphant. If your child is acting out, she should feel the consequences. As best you can, make the consequences a logical extension of the behavior.

Make changes

If you want to clear the clutter in your family life, you can't have a single family meeting in which you work out a few changes and hope for the best. Organization is not so much something that you do (although that's obviously important) as it is the way you choose to live your life. You need to incorporate decluttering and organization into your daily life.

Even with something as simple as toys or clothes or artwork from school, you can teach yourselves and your children to verbalize what's important and make choices based on priorities. Teach communication. Teach choice making. Teach them to honor and respect what's important and to have direction and purpose.

How do you teach all this stuff when you're just trying to get the laundry done and put food on the table every day? You do it by modeling. Your children watch and imitate everything you do. Value organization, control your environment, and live a decluttered life and they will too.

Use your goals to structure your day

Don't improvise daily. You should start every day with an image in your mind of how the day will go. In the morning, as you go about getting dressed and preparing breakfast, ask yourself these three questions:

- What do I need to get done today?
- What do I hope to get done today?
- What do I want from today?

Let the answers to these questions set your plan. Know that if you accomplish everything in your plan, you'll be satisfied with the day.

Stick to your guns

Don't let your child make decisions for you. Have your goals for the day in mind as you give your child structured options. Children grow increasingly independent every year of their lives, and you want them to keep growing and making choices. As they grow up, welcome their input in setting family goals. But don't let their whims and demands overrule you. You're the parent. Modeling the value and importance of a plan is a component of being organized. Talk to your child about what you have in mind and what you need to accomplish. Make wise choices and teach your children how to do the same.

Keep a calendar

If you feel like your life is a juggling act, the easiest way to keep all the balls in the air is to get serious about keeping your calendar. If you have two activities at once, specify which family members are going to which. This allows you and your partner to know who is doing what and allows you to organize your needs far in advance. Your children can use the calendar to easily find out what the week ahead holds for all of you. Encourage your children to add to the calendar from the day they say, "Let's ——— today," and when those "save the date" notes start coming in from school, you'll be glad they know what the calendar is for. By having well-ordered and logical systems in your home, you can teach kids the value and importance of a timetable and being organized. Place a notice board and calendar at their eye level. Use both and encourage them to do the same.

Implement routines

It's simple math: The more efficient you are, the more time you have. A little organization will go a long way to help streamline household routines. You should always shop with a list and plan meals for a week; that way you know what you need and what you are eating every night. You will be amazed at how this reduces stress and actually frees up time for you. If you buy the same basics over and over again, then type up a shopping list that you simply modify each week. If you have young children, keep a diaper bag ready to go. Clean it out and restock it each night and you'll find it much easier to get out the door in the morning. At night, while you're preparing dinner or your partner is doing the dishes, keep each other company by precutting snack foods and packing lunches.

Enlist help
Your kids are the cheapest labor around. Don't get me wrong, there are laws about this, but as my grandmother used to say, "Why buy the cow when you're getting the milk for free?" When it comes to doing things for the family—folding laundry, packing lunches, washing the car—your children are often excited to help (or "help," as the case may be). Involve them from the earliest age. Ask them to help with tasks at which they can easily succeed. Let them see how they can contribute to the smooth running of the house. Let go of the "it'll take too much effort to teach them" mentality or the "they can't do it as well as I can" idea. Settle for a little less than perfect, encourage the kids to pitch in, and be glad of the extra help. Putting away laundry, clearing the table, unloading the dishwasher, unearthing dirty clothes from under beds, using the vacuum cleaner—these are all tasks that kids can reasonably manage. Let them keep you company. Doing chores together is a wonderfully efficient way to spend family time and teach some great life lessons in the process.

Live in the present

When it comes to raising your children, it is enormously critical that you live firmly in the present. Childhood is fleeting. If you spend too much time focused on the past or the future, you will miss watching and helping your children grow up. Kids need you to be with them, and when you are with them, they need to be the focus of your attention. Remember what I said about multi-tasking. Be deliberate about the way you are spending your time. If you need to pay bills while you parent, make it clear that you are doing so and shouldn't be interrupted. But then when you're parenting, don't take phone calls or check e-mail.

Enjoy one-on-one time
No matter what your family structure, look for ways that each child can have time with a single parent. If you hadn't noticed, children crave parental attention. Spend some alone time with your child and you'll instantly see the joy and sense of individuality it gives him.

Be open to change
No matter how much effort you put into setting your goals for the day and figuring out how to achieve them, children are unpredictable. They get tired, they get cranky, and sometimes they get sick. Most of all, though, they are human with minds of their own! If an obstacle arises or they want to change the plans you made, don't be rigid; try to rework your plan to incorporate their needs and input. If you planned an activity for your child and he won't have fun doing it, there's no need to stick to the plan. If you're on your way to a fabulous butterfly exhibit, but your child is side-tracked by a newfound fascination with ants on the sidewalk, by all means scrap the museum and have an ant study session. On

the other hand, don't forget that you know more than your child, and if his changes impact the goals of your day negatively you need to be in charge. Use your better knowledge (rather than the power of your position) to make good decisions.

Be open to failure

Not everything has to go well. You walk into a friend's brunch and your child decides that she can't let go of your neck and sits on your lap for the entire meal. You take your child to the aquarium—he loves fish!—but he sees the giant octopus and screams in terror until you leave. Learn to roll with the thrill of parenthood. Don't get angry and don't let your child see your disappointment. Instead, talk about what happened and find a way to laugh about it. The point is to strive to enjoy and cherish your time together.

Face fears

When you decided to build a family, you changed your life. You changed your life in ways you never could have predicted because you didn't know who your kids would be or how being a parent would feel. Now you know. You know what your family life looks like today, and you've created an image of what you'd like it to look like in the future. But achieving that vision isn't going to be easy. You'll need to face some of your biggest fears on the way there.

Imperfection

I've already talked about being open to failure. Throwing the towel in on a trip to the grocery store is one thing, but admitting your own flaws is an entirely different ball of wax. You may not have an ideal disposition to be a parent. You may lack patience and feel like tying your kid's shoe instead of waiting the hour it seems to take him to do it himself. You may feel envious of the attention your spouse gives your children. You may feel conflicted or selfish about the time you wish you had to yourself. You may feel tired when you want to be energetic. You may feel bored when you want to feel charmed. You may yell at your children when you wish you could be calm. As a parent, your day is full of infinite opportunities to teach your children and to learn from them. It is also full of infinite opportunities to be less than the ideal parent who exists in your imagination. You make mistakes. I've worked with parents who are obsessed with what they "might have done" for their child and didn't. Like clutter, these "should-haves" can so fill your head with regret that it's tough to function. Don't be too hard on yourself—it's unlikely your kids will even remember most of those "mistakes" you feel you made. What's important is to do the best you can with what you have. Accept your weaknesses and find ways to work around them. Communicate with your children and remind them that you're only human. Show them how grown-ups can admit when they're wrong and move past their mistakes. Give your children your love in all its imperfection.

Loneliness
Your goal as a parent is to rear independent thinkers who will one day build their own lives. Your goal is not to rear fearful, immature whiners who are scared to venture more than a block away. Your children will grow up and, at some point, they will leave home. This is scary for two reasons. First, you worry if they will be safe out there in the big, unpredictable world. Second, after all this time spent rearing your children, you can lose track of who you are and not know how you will spend your time when they are gone.

Ah, this is why I urge you to work so hard to maintain a sense of who you are in the midst of rearing your children. Because if your identity is entirely wrapped up in being a parent, then one day, when they walk out that door, you will struggle to find yourself again. Let's face it, you'll struggle no matter what. But the sadness of an empty nest can and should be accompanied by a sense of curiosity and adventure as the center of your life shifts once again.

Paranoia

A client of mine saved every single article of clothing her children had ever worn. When I asked her why, she said, "The world's going to hell in a handbasket. I'm afraid that by the time my children have kids there won't be any more cotton." Hmm. I looked around her house. She wasn't saving paper bags for fear there would be no more trees. She was still purchasing plastics of all kinds—she wasn't afraid there would be no room for all the garbage. There were no emergency kits or gas masks. My client was sentimental about her children's clothing, plain and simple. I'm all for environmentalism, but I believe it should be incorporated into your daily life based on the information you have today. Don't use fear of catastrophe as an excuse for hoarding, and don't use it as an excuse for overprotection. Fear and clutter—they both overwhelm and paralyze us, rendering us unable to make reasonable decisions and live healthy, balanced lives. Assuming that the worst will happen may come from your instinctive desire to protect your children, but think about how it affects your parenting. You're modeling fear. You're presenting them with an unsafe, unreliable world. You're inhibiting their development of curiosity, confidence, and independence. Be a reasonable parent in a reasonable world.

Celebrate successes

Create time to enjoy the members of your immediate and extended family. Take interest in your children's lives and share yours with them. Find ways to appreciate one another. If you go on vacation, don't drag kids through activities that don't appeal to them. Look for ways to have fun together.

Celebration doesn't have to center around birthdays and holidays. Tell your family members what you appreciate about them at the moment it occurs to you. Thank your teenager for sharing stories about her friends. Let the whole family take pride in the work you've done to communicate, share, enjoy, and thrive in your lives together.

It's easy for things to become the focus of our lives and the indicator of success for our celebrations. The greater the event, the bigger the gift must be. Celebrate with a focus on experiences, not buying more things. Let your family see that what is valuable is the quality of time together and the strength of relationships, not the quantity of stuff that you can amass.

And then there's the stuff . . .

Families are messy. They drop crumbs everywhere. They generate loads of laundry. They have pets and friends and birthday parties and toys with more tiny pieces than there are stars in the sky. Sometimes the physical clutter is so extensive that it can interfere with your efforts to clear away the emotional clutter.

Let's talk about the fundamental changes that have to occur to make decluttering a way of life for your children.

1. *Happy to help*: Kids live as members of households and as such they need to understand from an early age that they're re-

sponsible for what they own and what they use. If your children are old enough to understand "put the blocks in the box," they're old enough to help. Make it clear that you expect your child to clean up the toys she uses. But do so without making it sound like a dreadful task. Don't start bargaining: "If you clean up your toys, I'll read you a book." Your child is not doing you a favor. Instead, channel Mary Poppins and say, "Let's get this puzzle cleaned up so you can read that book!" If your children need more motivation, challenge them to do it fast or well, and compliment their work once it is done.

2. *More stuff isn't more fun.* One surefire way to guarantee a stuff problem is to rear a child who is only stimulated by new purchases. Help your child learn to explore and create new uses for familiar toys. Educators talk about the benefits of open-ended toys—toys like building blocks that children can play with in infinite ways (as opposed to those annoying electronic toys where you push six buttons and you're done). I'm a fan of open-ended toys because children return to them again and again without getting bored. Be innovative. One of the best gifts I ever gave my young nephews was a stack of different-size cardboard boxes and some rolls of masking tape. Equipped with a box cutter, I followed their directions for what to cut where and helped them build spaceships, suits of armor, and even a castle. Bored children want new toys. New toys mean clutter. So look for toys that your child can explore in different ways for months, even years.

3. *Happy to grow up.* Clear out toys, clothes, and gear as your youngest child outgrows them. Don't sneak beloved toys out of the house in the dead of night and hope that your child forgets they ever existed. How would you feel if someone did that to you? You'd probably stop trusting the toy thief and keep a much closer guard on your remaining possessions. Instead, invite your child

to pick a few toys that he has outgrown. Together, pick a charity or friend who will be your beneficiary. If saying good-bye is hard, take a picture so that your child can preserve the memory in an album of outgrown toys. Let giving away toys be a ritual by which you celebrate your child's growth.

4. *Happy to give.* When you give toys away, don't miss the opportunity to instill in your child the value of giving. Even when he is young, he can enjoy the knowledge that he has made someone else happy. He can appreciate the fact that other children don't have the same advantages he has. One of my friends has established a ritual with his children where every birthday after they celebrate (and receive gifts) they go through their rooms and identify the items that they've outgrown and which can go to charity. I think it's a great tradition. Take your children to Goodwill or your local charity with the items that are being donated. Let them talk with the volunteers there so they understand where their donated item is going and who it will benefit. This is a wonderful lesson that promotes selflessness and instills an idea of giving that lasts a lifetime.

5. *Taking joy in a clutter-free home.* As items leave your home, talk to your child about what the benefits are. There is more room to play. Toys are easier to find. Your home feels organized and well-kept. Cleaning up shouldn't be a cruel, adult-imposed torture. It is an action your child undertakes because she understands what she herself likes about the results.

With these goals in mind, here is the process for freeing your family of the stuff that weighs you down and interferes with your vision.

- Create a vision for your children's rooms and the space they share with the whole family.

- Overcome obstacles that prevent you (and your kids) from letting go of items like toys, clothing, and artwork. If it doesn't serve your vision, it has to go.
- Commit time, even if it's only twenty minutes and two garbage bags every day. If you stop making purchases and purge a small area of your home for twenty minutes, you'll be surprised at how quickly you start to see changes. One bag for trash, and one for items to be donated. The results are cumulative. Just two of you, twenty minutes a day for a week—that's fourteen bags of trash and fourteen bags of items destined for Goodwill.
- Communicate with your children about your goals so they can understand and experience the benefits of being organized and build a foundation for a clutter-free life.
- Set boundaries. You only have the space you have—acknowledge and accept this. You can only have as many books as you have feet of bookshelf space. The same is true for toys, books, CDs, clothes, holiday decorations, and on and on and on.
- Make changes. Only by changing the role stuff plays in your life and the lives of your children will you be able to stop buying more things and let go of the clutter that impedes your life.
- Live in the present. Don't hold on to "memory clutter" that takes up so much room that you can't live your life. Don't hold on to articles in hope of one day living in a bigger home. Your life right now is the priority. Fix it by striking the right balance.
- Face fears. Sometimes clearing away the clutter with your children means that both or all of you have to learn to let go. Don't procrastinate by using your stuff to avoid dealing with reality.
- Celebrate successes. As you clear stuff away, the whole family will feel a sense of calm and renewal. Enjoy the space you now have to enjoy one another.

4

Money

Live for today *and* tomorrow

If a home I am working in has a clutter problem, there is a money problem not far behind. This is true without exception. We live in a culture that sends very clear messages about what we have and what we should have. The more successful we are, the more we should acquire—that's a sign of success, right? More is better— heck, if one is good, then two must be great, right? Don't pass up a bargain—if it's on sale, it has to be a fantastic deal, right? It's the ultimate irony to me that every year, especially around the holidays, we get media reports on the "health" of the American economy. The way that "health" is measured is by the rate of consumer spending. That's correct, the economy is only "healthy" if we're all out spending money on more stuff. By implication, if we happen not to be spending, then clearly we're not too well.

We are confronted daily with many conflicting messages: Buy, buy, buy. Save, save, save. Spend your tax rebate. Put money away for the future. The problem is compounded by the amount of "stuff" we see around us. Things are cheap, credit is easy to get, and we feel we deserve to have whatever we want, whenever we want it. But, and you know this, individually and as a nation we are spending more than we are earning, and sooner or later we'll have to pay the price of having whatever we want whenever we want it. It's easy to pull out the plastic, but not so easy to make the payments when gas, groceries, and the price of most other commodities is rising daily. If you have credit card debt and no idea how to get rid of it, you're not alone. But the fact that many of your fellow Americans are equally trapped in financial quicksand is no excuse, and it doesn't mean you're going to be okay. The stuff that chokes your home may well also be choking any chance you have for financial health. If this sounds like you, read on!

Dear Peter:

I want financial security. I want to stop renting and to have a secure retirement plan and a nest egg. But I haven't even been able to save the down payment required for a house. I live a comfortable life, buying myself plenty of little luxuries and clothing. It seems to be a discipline and priority problem much the same as the clutter problem that pervades my life.

Clutter takes us out of the present. The homes that I work in are usually filled with either "memory clutter"—the stuff that holds us strongly to an important person, an achievement, or an event in the past, or "I might need it one day clutter"—that's the stuff that we're keeping for that "just in case" moment sometime down the track. It's a wonderful thing to have important objects to remind us of beloved people or events from our past. It's useful to plan for an unpredictable future. However, people become so pre-occupied with what they have that they can't focus on what's most important—the here and now. Without a balance between these "past and future items," combined with a keen awareness of what is needed now, there cannot be peace and harmony in a home.

As with the stuff we own, so with the money we have. It's exactly the same.

Our culture urges us to become financially irresponsible the day we leave home or even before we fly the family nest. Credit card applications clutter your mailbox, promising that you can acquire all the trappings of adult life—cars! furniture! trips! dinners at fancy restaurants!—before you even have your first job. So we buy things. We buy whatever we want. Even before we start earning money, we've been so barraged with attractive advertising that we feel we have to go right out and spend. According to Nellie Mae, graduate students carry an average outstanding balance of over $8,000 on their credit cards. With employment comes easier access to money—either from an income or from one of the 1.3 billion credit cards burning a hole in our collective pockets. So our houses fill up—first with what we need, and then with stuff we don't need and, in fact, never use. If only we were able to save as well as we are able to spend.

Not so long ago I worked on a home that was floor-to-ceiling clutter. I estimated that there was more than $500,000 worth of purchases in the home, most still sitting untouched in the original shopping bags. When the unused items were sold—online and at a yard sale—the family made less than $20,000. The worst part of this story, however, is that the couple is in their sixties, in deep credit card debt, living off their home equity line, and with little savings or investments. Quite literally, the clutter is stealing this couple's financial security.

No matter how little or how much money you earn, managing

your money is simple. Yes, emergencies happen. Yes, jobs are lost. Yes, health insurance in this country is a real problem. Yes, living is expensive. I'm not saying you'll never end up in the hole. But there is a way out. There is a way to recover and there is a way to save. It all starts with cleaning up the mess you've made. Do you hide financial records from yourself or your partner? Do you leave mail unopened and bills unpaid for longer than you know you should? Do you feel guilty when you think about what you spend or what you owe? Do you feel scared when you think about your financial future? Do you buy on impulse and later regret the purchases? Do you spend with no idea of how much you have or what you owe? Do you have something as basic as a budget in place? Let's see just how much financial clutter you've got to clear away.

Quiz
Are Your Finances a Mess?

1. If you lost your job tomorrow, how long could you maintain the same standard of living without borrowing money?
    a. A couple of years, but I'd have to liquidate investments.
    b. Six months if I'm careful.
    c. I'd be in trouble from day one.

2. Do you know how much money is in your bank account?
    a. Yes, to the dime.
    b. Not exactly, but I always check my balance before paying bills or withdrawing.
    c. All I know is it isn't enough.

3. If you want to take a vacation this year, what will you do?
   a. I'll figure out how much I want to spend, then decide what I can afford.
   b. I'll go someplace I know I can afford so I don't have to worry about money once I get there.
   c. I'll put it on my credit card, enjoy the holiday, and worry about it later.

4. When it comes to the holidays or birthdays, how much do you spend on gifts?
   a. I have a set limit in mind for each person, and I stay on budget.
   b. I try not to go crazy. Mostly I shop in stores I can afford.
   c. I don't set a limit—I want to find gifts people love.

5. If you lost your current home and everything in it, what would you have left?
   a. Insurance money to replace most of what I had.
   b. Insurance money to keep me off the streets and some savings. It'd be hard, but I'd survive.
   c. A big pile of ashes, I guess.

6. How does the thought of investing your money make you feel?
   a. Excited—I check my investments daily.
   b. Nervous—it seems so risky. But I know it's the right thing to do.
   c. Paralyzed—I have no idea what I'm doing.

7. If you wanted to start saving more money, what would you do?

    a. Look at my bills and eliminate the luxuries that mean the least to me.

    b. Borrow money to pay off my credit card bills once and for all.

    c. Hawk my grandmother's engagement ring—or something similar.

8. What is most important to you?

    a. Feeling safe and secure.

    b. Leading a happy life from now on.

    c. Driving an expensive car and wearing the latest fashions.

9. If you got a raise tomorrow, you would:

    a. Invest it.

    b. Pay off my credit card bills and contribute the maximum to my 401(k).

    c. Splurge!

10. When you die, what will you leave your spouse, children, or heirs?

    a. A carefully planned estate.

    b. An insurance policy and some savings, if all goes well.

    c. Er, that's not my problem.

Are your finances a mess?

If your answers are mostly As:
You are a "Penny Pincher." You pay a lot of attention to the money in your life. You keep close track of how much you have, how you are spending it, and what you'd like to buy in the future. You are budget-minded and responsible, but at a price. Feeling safe and secure about your finances is important, but I want you to make sure you let yourself relax and have fun. Life is for living, not budgeting.

If your answers are mostly Bs:
You are a "Well-balanced Wallet." You believe in living your life and don't want to spend all your time counting pennies. You're making some efforts to save for the future, but you're also trying to live a good life today. I applaud your sense of priorities. Just make sure you don't have any credit card debt. That's a sure sign that you're overspending. And make sure you move forward with your plans to invest. There's no time like the present.

If your answers are mostly Cs:
You are a "Big Spender." You're all about instant gratification. You make impulse purchases without thinking about your priorities. You have few plans for the future. This is brash and risky. It's good to have fun. I'm glad you know how. But you can't expect your finances to sort themselves out. All this spending is going to come back to bite you on the ass if you get sick or when you want to retire one day. The good news is—you've come to the right place. Keep reading!

Imagine the financial life you want

Bills and paperwork can be overwhelming, especially if you're hiding bad spending habits behind disorganization. The first step to clearing your financial clutter is to set some goals. You work to earn money to live your life. Finance is about how you spend and save that money. Spending is about enjoying life today. Saving is for the future. Your financial goals should accommodate both. Let's get some organization into this by thinking about what you need and want today and in the future.

Dear Peter:

I feel very cluttered in my mind. I can't seem to think straight anymore. There is so much paperwork and bills, I just can't seem to get a hold of it or find the time to do it. I have five children and a new puppy. I'm just crazy, adding fuel to the fire. I hide all the paperwork everywhere. It's in bins, drawers, closets. Sometimes I can't find bills or important papers for my kids. I feel very overwhelmed; I've gained twenty pounds; I've become so unhealthy. I know all this, but cannot seem to get up and do anything about it. I'm afraid that it will take something drastic to make us change.

I hide bills and statements so my husband does not know how much I spend, and I really do not want to know how much I spend. I'm the cause of us going broke, but I don't stop. I just feel very jumbled at times, and I take it out on the family and my husband. It's a terrible feeling. Thanks for listening. I guess I should be going through some of my mail instead of writing to you.

Your emotional relationship with money

We aren't born knowing how to handle money. Our parents, peers, culture, and life experience guide us. Every household teaches different lessons, large and small, about the role of money in life. I know two families who lived next door to each other. In one house the children were taught to turn out every light in the house when they left home. If they left a light on, they had to put ten cents in a jar toward the wasted electricity. In the house next door, the children were taught to turn on all the lights before they left the house to ward off intruders, electric bill be damned! This may seem like a small difference in philosophy, but imagine what life would be like if the children from these two houses married.

My acquaintance Jon is a very successful investment banker. I can only imagine how much money he has socked away, but what I do know is that he has three lovely vacation homes in different parts of the country. He wears custom-made suits, owns several luxury cars, and eats at the finest restaurants in Manhattan. But join him on a trip to the grocery store and you'll see a different man. He agonizes over each purchase—should he really buy the yellow pepper that the recipe calls for when green peppers are half the price? Why purchase the fresh orange juice his wife has put on the shopping list when the frozen juice he grew up with is half the price? The Jon who emerges in the grocery store is fully defined by the financial upbringing his Depression-era parents gave him.

What are the lessons your parents taught you about money? Were they careful with how they spent money? Did they cut coupons and count pennies, but spend lavishly when it came to vacations? Are you imitating your parents' spending patterns or reacting against them? Were you taught to handle money? Did your parents give you an allowance and ask you to take responsibility for certain expenses? How old were you when you be-

came aware that there were certain things your parents could and couldn't afford? Did your parents keep you completely in the dark about how much money they had, how they decided to spend it, and what role it might play in your life as an independent adult? What effect have your peers had on your attitude toward money and spending? Do you spend more to keep up with them or do you see your friends making smart spending choices?

What is the emotional tenor of your relationship with money? Do you think of yourself as "bad at math" and leave the bill paying to someone else? Are you intimidated by investing? Do you feel entitled to certain material goods, regardless of how much they cost? Do you spend money impulsively and regret it later? When did you start doing this? Why?

How does your relationship with money have to change? Do you need to overcome fear? Do you need to educate yourself by reading a book or taking a class? Do you need to explore your sense of entitlement—where it came from and whether it is realistic—in order to bring your spending under control? You can't lose weight without eating fewer calories, and you can't save money without spending less. If you aren't happy with your financial situation, you'll have to remove emotion from the equation when it comes to your spending decisions. If you earn $100 and spend $90—no problem. If you earn $100 and spend $110—there's a problem. It's that simple!

Today's needs

How much of your income do you need to survive? Are you able to take care of those needs? Remember, you're just talking d' sustenance here. How much do you currently spend on clothing, and shelter? How much debt do you have? Is ' debt or "bad" debt? Good debt is money that you bor' something that will produce cash flow, like taking '

to purchase a home, which gives you a place to live, a tax advantage, and an asset that grows in value over time. Student loans also fall under this category—school increases your earning power. Bad debt is money that you borrow to purchase disposable items, often with a credit card. If you don't make monthly payments in full, you're effectively paying more for the items you purchased. What seemed a bargain the day you purchased it isn't such a deal when you're barely touching the principle and paying 25 percent interest on your credit card balance three months later.

Today's wants

Often when I am looking at the clutter in someone's home, the homeowner will exclaim with a lot of pride: "I'm a great shopper! I can find a bargain better than anyone else!" If you ever go shopping "just for fun," then every single thing you buy on one of those expeditions falls into this category—the stuff you want but don't need. You usually know when you're splurging. But in today's world, some of your luxuries have started to feel like necessities. If you're not successfully managing your money, spending responsibly, and saving for a rainy day or your retirement, then you're not entitled to a high-tech TV with cable service. That is a luxury. If you're not managing your money, then you're not entitled to expensive restaurants and prepared foods. Those are luxuries. If you're not managing your money, designer clothes, fancy cars, jewelry, and vacations are luxuries. If you have credit card debt and/or you're not managing your money, these are the areas you're going to have to examine for costs to cut. Notice some repetition here? If you're in a financial hole or struggling with your money and are serious about turning things around, these luxuries are the first things that have to go—no discussion!

Tomorrow's needs

Think about the major expenses that you know you'll have in the future, and imagine those that might take you by surprise. Will you need money to pay for a wedding—yours or your child's? Is there a chance you'll want to go back to school? Do you have children you hope will go to a private college? Do you own a home? How long will you be making payments on it? What maintenance is due? Will you need or want to move to a more expensive place?

As you think about your needs in the future, you must anticipate unpredictable circumstances. What if you have a serious car accident? You'll need insurance and money set aside to deal with medical expenses and lost income. What if something happens to your spouse? A parent? What responsibilities might you have and will you be able to afford them?

At some point, you will want to stop working, and at some point, whether you like it or not, you will have to stop working. Think about it. You won't want to move to a shack at age sixty-seven. You don't want to subsist on food stamps. You'll need to pay for health insurance, which is all the more expensive in your twilight years. You will still have monthly expenses, but your income will drop significantly. You'll want to have life insurance at rates that are locked in when you are young and healthy. You have to have savings if you want to sustain or improve your standard of living.

Tomorrow's wants

Are you living your dream, or do you fantasize about a future lifestyle with a higher pricetag? Do you wish you could afford more exotic vacations? Where would you like to live? Are you hoping to move to somewhere warm and sunny or to settle into a lush suburb? Would you like to leave your job for one that earns less money but is more fulfilling? Can you afford to do so? Do you anticipate retiring one day? How will you live? Will you take cruises? See a movie every day? Will you finally become a wine expert? What kind of car will you drive? Will you take some long-postponed vacations and pursue long-delayed hobbies? Well, guess what—you can't pay for your fantasies with play money.

A nest egg

I'm asking you to contemplate your needs, wants, hopes, and dreams and to translate those desires into dollars and cents. At the same time, I want you to make reasonable preparations for worst-case scenarios, when accidents, illness, job loss, family troubles, or (don't get me started) global warming wreak havoc on your finances. Money in the bank isn't just security, it's options. If you want a better lifestyle with a decrease in salary, if you want a better life for your family, if you want to be prepared for changes that crop up unexpectedly, your best bet is socking away the money that can open doors for you. The best way to feel safe and hopeful about now and the future is to create a comfortable nest egg.

Clear the clutter of unreal expectations

Before you lock the vision you just defined into place, I want you to think again. This will sound harsh, but most of us today have inherited an outrageous sense of entitlement. We have come to accept our high standard of living as normal, another of the many "rights" we assume as a citizen of this country. We think we deserve a big house just because we were born in or moved to this country. If we want it, we should be able to have it. This "self-first" mentality is relatively new and, I believe, inherently destructive. Think back just a generation ago. We don't carpool— we think each family member is entitled to a car. Did our grandparents have two cars? Did they pay for cable and multiple cell

Activity
Define Your Vision for Your Financial Life

Spend a little time thinking about your current financial situation: How much money you make, what you spend it on, and what your financial goals are. Keep those thoughts in mind as you complete this table.

Describe your current financial situation:

What I need to feel safe if my circumstances change (job loss, divorce, death in the family):

Major expenses that I face in the upcoming years (buying a home, kids' education, supporting parents in their old age):

What I need to survive when I retire:

What I want to enjoy when I retire:

Words that describe the financial situation you want to have:

- _____

- _____

- _____

- _____

- _____

Describe how you could achieve your financial goals:

What has to change to achieve your financial goals?

phones and the Internet and movie rentals? Did they have computers and digital cameras and printers? Did your grandmother
get manicures, massages, and highlights in her hair? How many
pairs of shoes did your grandfather own? The mindless consumption that I see day after day in the homes I work in is stagger-
ing. Consumption is perceived as our right, seemingly regardless
of the consequences. Our country is experiencing an explosion
of luxurious living that transcends economic class and it simply
cannot last. We can't spend with abandon, rack up debt buying
whatever we want, and not expect the bill to come due someday.
Someday soon!

So go ahead, envision your ideal financial life, but try to focus
on living your life, not filling it with objects. Remember that extra
stuff always comes at a cost. When you make a decision to spend
money today, you are responsible for that decision. If you spend all
your income on luxury goods when you are young, you'll pay the
price later. Try to appreciate what you have. It's not about depriv-
ing yourself, it's about striking a balance that enables you to spend
responsibly and live without the stress and anxiety that come with
financial problems. Curb the urge to acquire, and you'll have more
time and means to take pleasure in life.

Watch out for obstacles

People are scared of money. The easiest thing to do is to put your
paycheck in your bank account, spend what you spend, and hope
for the best. But the *wisest* thing to do is to be aware of in and out-
flow, to clear up bad debt, and to invest your savings so that it
grows over time. Unless you are in a financial crisis, you can clear
up the clutter around your finances little by little, without making
high-risk investments. There's nothing to be scared of, but fear is

the biggest obstacle to clearing financial clutter. Let's talk more about the other obstacles that stand in the way of your best financial future.

I-know-I-shoulds

Andrew is an architect in San Francisco. Andrew doesn't earn a lot, so he, his wife, and their three children save where they can, shopping at discount clothing retailers and driving an older-model car. He doesn't have money set aside for the children's educations, much less college, but he figures they'll find a way to make it work. On the other hand, Andrew loves new technology and his family always has the latest—from the latest-generation iPhones for him and his wife to fancy cell phones for his elementary school-age children. They love to dine out at the best new restaurants, with their children, and they enjoy going on expensive vacations every year. Andrew loves his life, which matches that of their social set. He knows he should resist these expenses, he worries, and he never goes into debt, but he watches their hard-earned savings drop a little each year.

My friend Eleanor is a successful freelance writer. I was chatting with her about her plans to buy a Manhattan apartment when it came out that she had all of her savings in a bank account. She had more than $60,000 just sitting there earning less than 1 percent interest, and most of it had been in the same account for over ten years! The long-term average return for the stock market is around 10 percent. Do you know how much that means she could have earned? Neither do I. I understood compound interest for five minutes in high school, and right at this moment I'm regretting that I didn't pay more attention so I could do the math. At any rate, I know she made a mistake, and she knew it, too. Too

nervous, too busy—whatever it was—she never got around to the very simple task of opening a brokerage account and buying a mutual fund or two.

If you know your finances aren't in shape, today is the day to start making changes. Forfeiting your $3.75 custom-brewed, extralarge, nonfat, no-foam latte every day for a year saves you more than $1,300. When it comes to spending and saving, small changes accumulate over time. Interest compounds (just don't ask me to do it for you) and that means money in your pocket.

Debt

Usually when I talk about clutter it's about the stuff that fills your home—the paperwork, all those extra clothes, the stuff in the garage or basement, and those unidentified items in black trash bags covered in dust under the bed in the spare bedroom. In this book, I've been talking about the clutter in your mind—doubts, fear, bad habits, poor communication, ingrained behavior—the obstacles that stand between you and the better life you could be living. Now, stop and think about this—debt itself is also a genuine obstacle that not only impedes your life, but also has the power to totally destroy it. It descends on you when you're young and foolish and accumulates faster than you can believe. Those appealing interest rates that entice you to get rich in the stock market make you poor when they're applied to your debt. If you have debt, my sympathies go out to you. Credit card companies really do take advantage of people when they are most vulnerable. *However*, now that you've gotten yourself into this mess, it's up to you to get yourself out of it. Don't hire a debt negotiator or a credit repair company. So many of them are scams that the FTC has a fact sheet recommending that consumers beware. Take responsibility. You can hire a reputable credit counseling organization.

Most of these are nonprofit, but there's little guarantee that their services are legitimate, and many of them have hidden fees. A referral through an institution, friends, or family is the safest way to go. Check www.ftc.gov for more guidance. The first and best step you can take to clean up your finances is to reduce, and ultimately get rid of your credit card debt. (In the next section, "Declutter Your Finances," I'll tell you how.)

Spending as leisure activity

When did recreational shopping become such a major participant sport in this country? It's so popular it has to be close to being included as an Olympic event! Anytime you head out to a mall, a shopping district, or a favorite store without a specific idea of what you need to buy, you are shopping just for fun. Think about it: Is spending money on clothes, music, electronics, or anything else one of your favorite activities? When you bring new items home, do they sit in the closet with the tags still on for weeks, months, even years? This is a really common sight in the homes I declutter. For many, many people in our consumer culture, recreational shopping has become an antidote for boredom or unhappiness. Shopping is the primary hobby of many people with whom I work. These people don't get as much pleasure from the items purchased as they do from the shopping itself. For most people who shop to shop, it is the addictive thrill of the purchase that keeps them going, the actual item acquired is secondary and is often forgotten quickly after being brought home. Unless you're loaded with cash, this pastime will get you in trouble, big trouble, and fast! The constant purchasing not only fills your home with the clutter of unused items, but it also drains your bank account and drives up your credit card bill. The clutter of the stuff and the clutter of the debt make an impressive—and daunting—team.

Lack of prioritization

If you don't have a major shopping problem, there's no need to go cold turkey. You just need to make smart choices about when and how you spend your money. There are infinite nice things you can purchase. How do you know when to stop if you don't have a sense of what you can afford or how to stay on budget?

Fear and denial of the future

Planning for your future doesn't mean living like a monk today and saving for a plush retirement. Planning for your future means safeguarding yourself and your family against financial collapse if all doesn't go as planned. You need an emergency fund of easy-to-access savings that you can rely on if you're out of work for six months (longer if your employment is unreliable). You need disability insurance and a will. It's tough to set this money aside when it doesn't buy tangible goods. Being in a car accident would be bad enough. You don't want it to destroy you financially as well as physically.

Dear Peter:
I only deal with the clutter in a crisis situation. For example, the other day my husband wanted me to check on a bill. I spent the whole morning going through papers when I should have been doing something else, only to discover that I had created another mess, which in turn created a lot of stress and negative feelings. I bet there are times when I have handled a piece of paper a half dozen times before it finds its rightful home.

Activity
What's Getting in the Way of
My Ideal Financial Situation?

Reviewing the sections above, write down the obstacles that stand in the way of achieving the financial health you're after.

• _____

• _____

• _____

Paperwork procrastination

Whenever I declutter people's homes, it's paperwork, especially mail, that's a major issue. The only way to know how much you have, how much you owe, how much you're saving, and how much you can spend is to open those envelopes, pay those debts, and file those bills.

Declutter your finances

Commit time

It can be overwhelming when you start clearing up your financial situation. How do you even know where to start? Whenever I face a situation of any kind with a client—be it physical clutter, diet, or money management—that is completely out of control, I like to begin with a Quick Purge to bring some of the most daunting mountains down to size. When it comes to your finances, you're not going to start by purging—you don't want to throw away any important documents. Instead, you'll do a Quick Count. This is a one-time investment in your financial future and I need you to devote time to it. Set aside at least half a day and be prepared to work until you've finished taking stock of your current financial situation.

The purpose here is to get a clear snapshot of where you stand financially—what you have, what you own, and what you owe. This may be frightening, but the clarity that comes from having a clear understanding of your financial situation is more empowering than you might imagine.

Communicate

Now that you have this snapshot of where you stand financially, it's time to figure out where you want to go. Remember that very few people have the ability to buy whatever they want whenever they want it. You need to strike a balance between meeting your financial responsibilities, enjoying your life today, and investing in your goals. Understand what's important to you and make choices based on your priorities. If you are married or in a long-term relationship, do this with your partner.

Shared goals

When you fall in love and decide to spend the rest of your life with someone, the first conversation you have usually isn't, "So, are you fiscally responsible?" Consequently, money is one of the earliest and biggest problems to crop up in many long-term relationships. Money is one of those key issues, like child rearing, that people have deep beliefs and views about. Rarely do couples have the same attitude about money. Most of us don't find money

Activity
Quick Count

1. Clear a space.
2. Gather documents. I want you to gather your most recent financial statements—your bank accounts, credit card statements, loans, and unpaid bills. For some of you, this will be harder than others. If the statements are buried in piles of paper, don't worry about anything else in that pile right now, just dig out what you need and deal with the rest later. If your accounts are online, either print out a statement or write the balance on a piece of paper. Now, put all your statements on the table in two piles:

A. What You Have	B. What You Owe
Savings accounts	Outstanding credit card bills
Checking accounts	Loans (mortgage, car, student)
401(k)	Other unpaid bills
Investment and brokerage	Any other debts
Other investment accounts	
Down payment on home	
Other (car, house, furniture, jewelry, and any other major assets)	

3. Tally it up. Add column A together and write the total down. Do the same with column B. If you subtract what

you owe from what you have, you'll get your net worth, but I'm not really so concerned with that. Your net worth is an indicator, but it's not a lot of help in planning a financial strategy. Instead, what I want you to do is—

4. Evaluate your situation. Look at the two columns in front of you. These columns are a snapshot of your financial life. One column is what you've saved and the other is what you've spent. But they are not good and evil. The first column represents all the efforts you've made to plan for your long-term goals. The second represents all the living you're doing right now. It's important to have a good quality of life, but how you're living today influences your future. Spending money on your education is an investment in the future—buying another pair of black shoes is not. So when you look at these two columns, I want you to be honest with yourself. Is this the record of someone who overspends, or someone who is smart and careful with money? Is this the record of someone who is just hoping it'll somehow work out, or is it the record of someone who has taken responsibility for the life they're living?

the most romantic topic of conversation, but the problems that come with financial clutter are real and worth clearing away. Otherwise they can grow to be as painful and out-of-control as any home overrun with all those things someone inherited from his grandparents and just can't seem to let go.

If your attitudes toward spending are wildly diverse from your partner's, the best way to resolve them is on paper. Instead of criticizing money choices, decide on your financial goals together. You need to have a shared vision for your finances in the same way you need to have a shared vision of the life you want. In both cases, the vision comes *before* you decide how best to deal with the clutter. Calculate what you need to save to reach your vision. Once you establish your goals, you will know how much money you can spend on luxuries. Only at that point should you start to discuss what level of spending is reasonable and how to manage it.

Activity
Set Financial Priorities

With your financial standing—the self-evaluation you just did—in hand, set your priorities. Use the example below for inspiration.

My financial priorities for this year:

1. Move to a place with a lower rent.

2. Pay off credit cards with extra rent money in the next six months.

3. After credit card debt is paid off, maximize my 401(k).

4. Save up enough to buy a new car.

That's it. Clean and simple. Now set your own priorities.

My financial priorities for this year:

1. _____

2. _____

3. _____

4. _____

5. _____

Spending quirks

Every household has spending contradictions. You buy discount toilet paper but subscribe to three hundred cable channels. You only buy clothes on sale but drink expensive wine when you go out to dinner. You drive around looking for the best gas price but enjoy extravagant vacations. You spend an hour on the phone getting a fifteen-dollar late fee eradicated, but you indulge in expensive art. It's okay to have spending quirks, but you should acknowledge and own them. And if you're in a partnership, you should both be onboard with your spending choices. Now is the time to talk them through.

Spending secrets

Do you buy new shoes and hide the price tags from your husband? Does your wife know how much that new television cost? Hiding money secrets may not feel like deception because you never shared your expenditures with your spouse before you got married. But if you keep secrets, you need to ask yourself why. Why are you lying to the person who should be your closest confidant? What are you afraid of? You may enjoy the expensive dress you bought behind your husband's back, but what is it *costing*

Activity
Assess Your Financial Compatibility

With your partner, take this list and write how much you think is reasonable for your household to spend on each item. Compare the results.

Item	Partner A	Partner B
A night out		
A week-long vacation		
A winter coat		
A car		
A week of groceries		
A pair of shoes		
A wedding present for a family member		
A wedding present for a work colleague		
A week of preschool		
A child's music class		

you? Now is the time to come clean and not compound spending problems with deceit. Either you have the money to afford your purchases, or you don't. If you truly plan to grow old with your partner, you need to find common ground in terms of how you are going to do that. The first step is to know and agree on where your hard-earned money goes.

Set boundaries

I've said that in your physical space, your relationships, your job, and your family you need to set limits. The same is true for your money. If you don't honor and respect your relationship with your money, that relationship will eventually sour and, like the clutter in your home, become overwhelming, suffocating, and even paralyzing.

The concept of a budget is one that terrifies many people. They're worried about the restrictions a budget will place on their spending. But budgets, like room planning or deciding what will best fit into a space, are actually a step toward greater freedom rather than less. In your decluttered home, I ask you to set boundaries by only keeping the amount of stuff with which you can comfortably live the life you want to live. In relationships, those boundaries are more abstract and personal. At work, you need to establish boundaries that separate your work life and your home life. When it comes to money, you need to set boundaries that help you balance your needs and desires in the present and your needs and desires in the future. With clear boundaries, there are no unwelcome financial surprises and your financial situation is clearly laid out. This type of financial organization frees you from many of those nagging worries and concerns about the unknown.

That said, I'm not a fan of keeping a budget that is so meticu-

lous that the budget becomes a source of stress and
budget should be a tool to help you manage your mon
consensus on what is reasonable spending, and track the
cial health of your family. If the budget becomes an end in it
it's unlikely that you'll have any commitment to sticking to it r
long.

Why not give it a shot? Here let's create a one-time budget, a
budget for grown-ups.

Activity
Set a Grown-up Budget

Add up your baseline monthly expenses. These are costs you have every month: mortgage or rent, gas and electric, water, phone, cable, insurance, and so on.		$
Add necessary expenses, like gas or other transportation charges.	+	$
Take any ongoing necessary expenses like child care, medical expenses, parking or tuition, and school fees. Figure out the annual cost, then divide by twelve to get the monthly cost.	+	$
Total all your necessary expenses. These are your fixed monthly costs.	=	$
Monthly income:		$
Subtract your fixed monthly costs from your monthly income.	−	$
The remainder is your discretionary money.	=	$

Before you get too excited about how much you have
, consider this: You haven't factored in food, clothing,
s, or emergency funds. Now I want you to examine the last
e or more months of credit card bills and bank statements to
e how much "discretionary" money you're actually spending on
a monthly basis. Is it more than you have to spend? Are you just
breaking even?

Decide how much of your discretionary money you want to
save each month. Decide where you want to save it (direct deposit
to a money market account works), and put it there the day you
get your paycheck. Then you have a general sense of how much
money you have to spend for the rest of the month while guaranteeing that you're putting money away to pay off debts or build a
nest egg. If your current spending rate is in line with your goals,
great. If not, choose some cuts that will put you in the right range.
Instead of counting every penny you spend, you're making a lifestyle adjustment.

Tip

Use online calculators or a one-time financial planner to figure out how much you need to set aside every month in order
to retire. Direct deposit that money into your savings (or
whatever account works for you) every payday.

Break the shopping habit

If you always joke about being a shopaholic, or you know that
you have a real shopping compulsion, it's time to start taking
the problem seriously. Start by keeping a shopping journal. Track
when and why you make your purchases, and look for trends. Do
you shop to reward yourself? Do you shop when you're lonely?

Stressed? Do you always shop with the same friend or friends? Can your shopping companions afford more expensive stores than you can?

The idea of spending money to save money is one that I encounter often. Something is a bargain—or a "real bargain"—so you'd be crazy to pass it up, right? You bring the "great deal" home and, because you don't need it right away, you put it away in a cupboard or closet and there it sits. Here's the bottom line—as long as there are shops and markets and malls (or the Internet), there will *always* be another bargain, another sale, another deal. My grandmother was so right when she said that you can go broke saving money. Leave the deals where they are, keep the clutter at bay, and put a little something in the bank.

Once you've identified the triggers that compel you to shop, look for new activities to fill those needs. Can you fill the empty time with equally fulfilling activities, like pursuing new hobbies, exercising, or spending time outside? Try imposing a six-month moratorium on shopping. Nothing except the bare essentials (food, cleaning supplies, toilet paper) comes into the house. It's a challenge, but not only will you see how few purchases you truly need, you'll jump-start your savings.

Look to the future
Remember, it's not guaranteed that you'll be able to work until the day you die. And even if you could, who wants to? Even if your aunt Ruth has promised to leave you millions, there's just no guarantee. Take responsibility for your own future. No matter how young and in debt you are, your plan must include saving money. You may not be able to start doing so today, but plan to get there. You can send me a letter from your lavish retirement home in the south of France to thank me—include a round-trip ticket for me to come visit, too!

Activity
Make Smart Choices

Ask yourself these questions before you make any purchase:

Does this item move me closer or farther away from the vision I have for the life I want?

Do I need this?

Will I value it?

Can I afford it?

What will it replace or what will I get rid of to make room for it?

What do I hope this item will do for me now and in the future?

Make changes

Hold the idea of the life that you want in your mind as you work through the process. Just as clutter doesn't appear overnight and won't disappear overnight, your financial problems can't be solved in a day. Here are all the steps you should follow to clear your financial clutter in order of priority. Just cross off the ones that don't apply to you and you'll have your plan.

1. *Clear away the paper piles.* The only way to face the reality of your financial situation is to start with a clean slate. Your financial life will not take care of itself. Look to the place in your home where you currently manage your financial matters and ask yourself: Does the financial management of my life have a high prior-

ity? Show that you give priority to managing your finances by establishing a place in your home for paying your bills, keeping financial records, and managing the money aspect of your life. You give priority to what you think is important.

2. *Get out of credit card debt.* Hands down, credit card debt is the most destructive type of clutter you can have in your life. No matter what your financial goals are, the first change anyone should ever make is to overcome credit card debt. In case you didn't notice, credit cards have the highest interest rates around. They are ruinous. The interest that you're paying on that debt is higher than the interest you might earn on even the best investment. So before you invest a single dime, you need to work to pay off your credit cards once and for all.

Experts agree that the best—and possibly the only—way to pay off credit card debt is by yourself, little by little. Gather all your credit card statements together. For each card, write down the total amount you owe, the minimum monthly payment, and the interest rates.

Card	Total Owed	Minimum Monthly Payment	Interest Rate

Pick the card with the lowest interest rate and destroy all the other cards. From now on this will be the only card you use, and you will only use it for *essential* purchases until you have paid off all of your debt. Start paying with cash.

Add up your minimum monthly payments. At the very least, commit to meeting them every single month. If you miss a payment, your interest rate goes up, your credit score goes down, and it will be harder and more expensive for you to borrow money in the future. On top of paying the monthly minimum, you should commit a minimum amount toward reducing the principal owed every month without ever, ever letting your car or house payments fall behind. I'm sorry, but I didn't say this would be easy. Just keep in mind how much further your paycheck will go when you're no longer paying such enormous interest fees on your debt. The climb out of credit card debt can be one of the toughest you'll make, but it's worth the focus and willpower to achieve it.

Decide on an additional amount that you will contribute to your debt every single month. Make it as big as possible. Remember, making this payment every month will bring down your minimum monthly payments. How exciting is that? Still, this is the hard part. You're in debt for a reason—it's been hard for you to save. Think of this as a serious money diet. Only allow yourself essentials until all the debt is gone. No shopping. No birthday presents. No restaurant meals. No travel. If you have credit card debt, you've been living beyond your means. It's that simple. Now it's time for the overspending to stop and the underspending to start.

Attack the cards with the highest interest rates first. As you embark on paying them off, try to get your rates reduced. Call the credit card companies one by one. Tell them you're pleased to be a customer, but you would like them to lower your rate so you don't have to take your business elsewhere. Even if you are never going to use those cards again (which I hope you don't), go ahead and make that call. Don't sound like a desperate, broke debtor. Remember, you're paying these folks lots of money. You're calling them as a customer who is looking for better service.

Even if you don't succeed in getting your rates down, you have a plan. You're paying the monthly minimum every month, and paying down the maximum you can every single month. Stick with it. Do. Not. Shop. Imagine how wonderful it will feel to put that monthly minimum into a savings account instead of into a credit card company's deep pockets.

3. *Cut spending now.* Don't spend money you don't have. That sounds like pretty simple advice, right? But simple's not always easy. When it comes to discretionary spending—the small spending choices you make on a daily basis—there is a basic rule: *Don't spend money you don't have.* At first, you will have to work hard to keep your wallet in your pocket, but after a while you will realize that this choice has become habit. You'll benefit twice: less clutter and more money.

4. *Start setting money aside for the future.* Unless you've been given a year to live, you need to be saving for the future. If you aren't saving, you need to make changes. I don't want you to feel like you're scrimping to get by. I want you to enjoy your life. But spending your way into stress, sleepless nights, collection calls, and maybe even bankruptcy isn't worth the costs. Money isn't the only way to enjoy life. You need to find a way to thrive without overspending. Don't count on things changing without your taking action. Let me say that again: *Don't count on things changing without your taking action.* They never do. You can buy all the lottery tickets you want, but meanwhile, learn to enjoy living within your means so you don't feel the paralyzing stress of financial clutter.

You spend too much money on stuff you just don't need. This may sound like a bold statement—I've never met you. But I'm

Activity
What Am I Willing to Give Up?

Make a list of the expenses you're willing to sacrifice and how much you expect to save on each. Deposit the total amount directly from your paycheck into savings *before* you have a chance to spend it on anything else. If you are in a relationship or have a family, do this together.

Item	Cost	x Number per Month	Total
Takeout dinner			
Morning coffee and pastry			
Movies			
Weekday lunches			
New clothes			
Shoes			
Cosmetics			
DVDs or music			
After-work drinks			
Travel			
Total savings per month:			

confident that it is true for 90 percent of the people who buy this book. You didn't get where you are—feeling like your life is cluttered and out of control—without bringing too much stuff into your home and your life. The best way to break your shopping habits is by going cold turkey. Just stop. Keep remembering that you really need very little to be happy and they don't sell happy at the store. Shopping is not the only recreation in the world. Get your family or friends involved in other activities. Challenge one another to find other ways to entertain yourselves. I'm confident you can do it.

5. *Invest your money wisely.* The first investments you should always make are those that you can do with pretax dollars. Why? Because money that you contribute to a 401(k), an IRA, or another retirement plan doesn't count as income for tax purposes. In fact, you won't pay taxes on it until you retire. That means more money sitting in your account, growing over the years. If your employer offers a 401(k), you should max it out. Open an IRA and contribute the maximum every year. If you have children, open 529 college saving plans, which aren't subject to capital gains taxes, for each of them and contribute the most you can every year and encourage the grandparents to contribute cash (they'll have to do it through you) rather than bring more of the same toys every time they visit. Bear in mind that none of these retirement investments is liquid. Before you invest, make sure you have emergency funds to carry you for several months in case of illness, injury, or job loss.

6. *Balance your portfolio.* Don't be scared of your money. You don't need to be a financial wizard to invest your money so that it grows over time. The key words are "over time." All investments have some level of risk, but over the long term, the stock market has only grown. What that means is that if you are truly saving for a retirement that isn't on the imminent horizon, you can bear

some risk. Why? Because you won't be withdrawing the money for a long time, so if the market falls, you won't feel the loss. By the time you need the money, it will have bounced back, and, by the miracle of compound interest, the more years you've had money in the stock market, the more the amount that you have will have grown.

Where to go for help

If you know nothing about individual companies, then don't buy individual stocks. Instead, opt for low-fee mutual funds that aggregate a number of stocks. Choose a diversity of funds. I'm not a financial adviser. There are plenty of books, websites, and magazines that tell you how to balance your portfolio to include small-cap, large-cap, domestic and international stocks, and bonds. You've probably heard of the big ones: *Money* magazine, MSN Money, CNNMoney, Motley Fool (www.fool.com). Don't write these off as resources for "other people," people who already know about finance. All of these sources provide basic information for new investors. At the very least, you can research a portfolio balance that makes sense for you, and then review your portfolio at the end of each quarter and adjust it so that the balance of investments stays the same. You can do that, can't you?

If you're ready to take it to the next level, discount brokerage houses like Vanguard offer onetime financial advice with a flat fee (for Vanguard, the fee is $1,000 per year if you have less than $100,000 invested). Your bank probably offers advisory services. Or ask friends to recommend a money manager who can make onetime recommendations or handle your investments for you. Get some sound financial advice. Understand what you're doing. If unsure, ask lots of questions until you feel comfortable and informed. Capital gains taxes can affect your profit significantly, so don't buy and sell willy-nilly. You need to factor in how long you've held an investment.

Live in the present

I always talk about being where you are. Being present. Being in the now. So what's with all this talk about putting money away and saving for the future? Well, for one thing, most of the money people spend is on unnecessary items that only add to the clutter in their homes. Those items promise you a life that seems out of reach—one in which you are beautiful, rich, even wildly successful. But saving for retirement is the best action you can take toward achieving that out-of-reach life. Of course, saving for retirement isn't all that matters. I do care about the quality of your life right now. If saving for a reasonable future takes a toll on your life today, I want you to think carefully about what the true cost is. What are you sacrificing? What should you be sacrificing? How can you make up for that value? Again, it's about striking a balance that works for you.

Live within your means

Why do you spend more than you can afford? I don't buy it when people plead dumb, saying they just don't know how to manage their money. Change comes with choice. You have to make the choices instead of letting the situation or circumstances choose for you. I have great confidence in the innate wisdom and ability of people—I see it constantly and at the most surprising of times. I believe in you and your awareness of your own circumstances. If you get bills you can't pay every month, but you still buy new clothes or the latest electronic gadget or cell phone, something else is going on. Some part of you feels entitled, like you deserve to live at a certain level. Maybe you grew up with certain luxuries and you have trouble giving them up. Maybe you went without as a child and you don't want your own family to suffer the same sense of deprivation. Maybe you're trying to keep up with the Joneses, and the Joneses are out of your league. Whatever the reason, you are out of touch with reality. The more stuff you buy, the more you bring into your home, the further you move from what is real. That lack of connectedness has a real cost. It can be tough to stay on a budget when your friends are eating at expensive restaurants, driving the latest-model cars, and wearing pricey clothes. It can be hard to resist your children's desires when you want them to have every opportunity. I'm sympathetic, truly I am. But I insist that you balance the value of those items today against what they will cost you tomorrow. In our society, the passage of time directly affects how much money we have. Debts grow over time. Investments grow over time. The sooner you take control the better, even if it means inviting your friends over for pizza instead of shelling out for the four-star restaurant. So you might have to swallow a little of your pride in the process—is that so bad? You can even try being open about your choice. Many people are struggling with their finances. You might just be surprised at how well others respond.

Vacations

Most of your vacation costs are the air travel and hotel accommodations. There are many ways to cut these costs and still take a relaxing, rejuvenating break from your work life.

- Let airfare be your travel agent: buy tickets far in advance or to the place with the best rates.
- Stay close to home. Save on the airfare by being a tourist in your own town or city, or traveling within driving distance.

- Visit friends who live someplace cool. Just make sure you're entirely welcome, don't overstay, and splurge on a generous host gift for them.
- Rent an apartment with a kitchen. You'll save enormously by not eating every meal out.
- Treat yourself at home. Eat out and have massages in your hometown every day for three days. Go visit those local attractions that others come to your city to see but you never do. You'll spend far less than you would for a week out of town.

Eating out and takeout

With half of all meals now eaten outside the home, we are spending more money than ever on fast food and restaurant meals. Even the least-expensive restaurants cost more than preparing food at home. Find substitutions that do what restaurants do for cheaper:

- A romantic dinner. A picnic is the most romantic homemade meal around. If the weather isn't right, have a picnic on your living room floor. If your living room won't cut it, choose certain nights to put a special romantic spin on dinners at home. Find a new menu online, light candles, and save the dishes for the morning.
- Eating out. Eating out costs more than eating in. And it doesn't necessarily save time. If you prepare your food at home you can use the "in the oven time" to do other things, like talk to your kids or partner, pay bills, decompress, or walk the dog. You saved money and bought yourself some time. If it's the effort of cooking the meal that overwhelms you, try buying prepared, or nearly prepared, foods at the grocery store occasionally. Just make sure they are healthy and that you aren't spending all your money on short term convenience.

Clothes and furnishings

- Impulse shopping. If you want to save money, the first activity that has to go is shopping for pleasure. Of course, it's always fun to have something new, but don't buy a new TV just because you see one on sale. If your TV works, do you really need a new one? Are you shopping to fill the hole of unhappiness? Are you hoping that something new will change your life? Is shopping a way of avoiding being home or facing reality? Every time you have the instinct to add something to your cart, stop and pause. Think about what you're about to do.

- Children's clothes and toys. Even if you're a very careful spender, you might find yourself splurging on your kids. You love them. You want the best for them. Maybe buying things for them makes you feel like a better parent. Maybe it gives you a sense of control. Maybe it makes you feel better about not having enough time with them. Maybe you buy things for your children in order to answer one of your own needs or to fulfill your own dreams—that you never had enough money growing up to get what you wanted as a kid. Or you want your kid to be cool because you weren't. Perhaps the only reason you indulge your children is because you want to (temporarily, it turns out) silence the endless begging and pleading. Maybe you are caught in the idea that more is better and have a misguided sense that the more things you give your kids the more you love them. There's an endless supply of cute clothes, shoes, and toys out there. Something is always on sale. The best way to control spending on your children is to stay out of the stores. Period. Don't buy for your child's future sizes or tastes. You never know how fast she'll grow or how his taste will evolve. Wait until he or she gets there. And when they do, I guarantee there'll be another bargain and another adorable outfit waiting just for you! Solicit hand-me-downs from friends and family and shop secondhand stores when a need arises. Kids grow so quickly that there are often some lightly used garments that barely made it out of the dresser.

- Gifts. I'm all for gifts when they are unique or useful and inspired. What I can't stand is gift giving for the sake of it. If you have the kind of relationship with your friends and family where they know what your financial situation is, then it is perfectly acceptable to substitute a thoughtful, handwritten card for a birthday or holiday gift. It really *is* the thought that counts! If you can't keep your gifts appropriate to your wallet, don't give anything at all. If the holidays are an over-the-top gift exchange, propose that only children receive gifts, or implement a Secret Santa drawing, where each family member chooses a name out of a hat and gives only to that person.

Big-ticket items (electronics, home improvements)

I am sorry, but if you are serious about saving money, you just don't need a flat-screen TV. Nor does your thirteen-year-old son need the latest iPod, laptop, or cell phone. Yes, these luxuries improve your quality of life, but I question whether they improve it significantly. Put differently, is the sticker price worth the cost to you and your family? You can watch the same programming on a lesser TV. You can listen to the same music on a less-expensive MP3 player. Don't be an early adopter. Wait until the digital camera you want is cheaper. TVs get less expensive every year. All of these items come with a cost to you and your family's financial stability.

Home improvements can be necessary, like a new roof, or optional, like landscaping or renovating. Renovating costs add up fast, so keep in mind a basic rule of renovation. Take what the contractor tells you, then assume it will take double the time and double the budget—it's a law of the universe. Stick to necessary changes, avoid financing any renovation through your credit cards, and stay within your budget. In the excitement of improving your home, it's easy to overcapitalize. Get some solid advice and don't lose your head. Set a budget, look your contractor in the eye, tell him the figure, and—come hell or high water—stick to it. Even if it means some part of your initial project has to wait till next year.

Grocery bills

When it comes to grocery bills, you can't just buy cheap bulk foods. Healthy choices (which we'll explore in the next chapter) are sometimes more expensive, but they have cost benefits. Junk food affects your health and well-being and, ultimately, your ability to perform well at your job and your kids' ability to do their best at school. Junk food is not the path to happiness and a long life. If you eat healthy, balanced meals, you'll feel satisfied. You'll be a healthier weight, you'll live a healthier life, you'll feel more attractive, and you'll spend less money trying to find clothes that don't make you look fat. Buying and cooking your own meals with whole foods means healthier meals and a healthier future. I've written a whole book on the connection between the weight in your home and the weight on your hips. Check out *Does This Clutter Make My Butt Look Fat?: An Easy Plan for Losing Weight and Living More* for strategies and techniques for tackling this area.

We'll talk about clearing the clutter in your diet in the next chapter. For now, all I ask is that you don't waste money on anything that promises to make you thin. Invest in a long and healthy life, don't splurge on the easy, empty, quick-fix promises that you're bombarded with every day. Instead, take the time to plan meals that truly nourish and sustain your family.

Small expenses (lunch, coffee, movies, magazines)
Little luxuries are often the most painless cutbacks to make. But there's no point in making these sacrifices if you don't end up with the savings to show for it. If you decide to eliminate your daily latte, then put aside the cost of however many lattes you used to have and make weekly or monthly deposits in a savings account or a "drip" fund, stock funds that often let you make investments of as low as ten dollars. (Drip—what better name for a fund holding your coffee savings?)

No real bargains
Remember my grandmother, who used to say that you can go broke saving money? I've said it before and I'll say it again: There's no such thing as a bargain. Instead of looking for the best deal, I want you to practice *mindful* spending, valuing quality over quantity. Cheap things don't last. They either perform badly or soon need to be replaced. That's how you can go broke trying to save money.

Face fears

Just like the clutter in your home, it's easy to ignore your financial situation. Over time those numbers stop feeling meaningful. Maybe you buy lottery tickets or hope you'll get a windfall from the lonely, childless widow next door or long-lost Uncle Bill who moved to Florida twenty years ago. But denial doesn't work forever. You need to take control of your money while you still can. You need to take responsibility. Money may not interest you, but you need it to live. You need it to create certain (though by no means all) aspects of your ideal life.

Clearing your debt—just like clearing any clutter that stands between you and the life you want—should be a priority. Make it one. Keeping your spending secret from your partner is another form of denial. You think if your little gambling habit or shopping problem is never acknowledged, then it doesn't exist. Wrong! The longer you deceive your partner, the harder it will be to restore trust. Shame is hard to endure, but the damage that dishonesty wreaks on a relationship is far worse. Cut your losses and clean up your mess sooner rather than later.

Assess your risk endurance

My onetime colleague, Lynne, had two grandfathers who were both lawyers. They both worked for the government, so neither had an enormous income. One grandfather was a savvy investor. He invested all of his savings in the stock market and real estate. The other avoided risk, especially when it came to his money. He put all of his savings in treasury bonds, with a low but reliable interest rate. At the end of their lives, the grandfather who invested was a millionaire. The conservative grandfather left his wife with a small apartment, a pension, and barely enough savings to get her through the next thirty years she went on to live without him. Riskier investments have greater returns. Get advice that helps you know what level of risk you're financially and emotionally ready to handle.

Plan for unforeseen circumstances

You could lose your job. Your home might burn down. You could be in a severe car accident. A family member may become suddenly ill. You will most certainly die. Thinking through these possibilities isn't doomsaying, nor does talking about misfortunes cause them to occur. Dispense with the superstition and be realistic. You need to protect yourself and your loved ones from financial ruin if the unexpected occurs.

If you're the primary breadwinner for your household, consider how long it might take you to find a job. If it will take you six months, then how much money do you need to have readily available in a money market or other accessible bank account? You should try to have enough money to cover six months of living expenses. If you are self-employed, you need to think about disability insurance. If you think you don't need it because you're in perfect health, think again. According to the American Council of Life Insurers, nearly one-third of all Americans will suffer a serious disability between the ages of thirty-five and sixty-five. And as for life insurance, if your untimely death would put your family in dire straits, don't live in denial. Take care of them. By all means, leave a will. An estate planner can help you make sure your assets aren't tied up in probate while your loved ones live on bread and water. And be sure to update these policies if you marry, divorce, have children, or remarry. I know it's hard to contemplate these hardships, but don't let your emotions clutter your priorities. If you care about the people closest to you, you'll spare them cleaning up your mess when you're incapacitated or, you know, dead.

Celebrate successes

Needless to say, I don't want you to celebrate cleaning up your financial clutter by throwing the party of your life. The rewards that come from taking control of your financial future and clearing the financial clutter from your life are significant. Some of them only kick in when you're sixty-five, but some of them come earlier—the sense of relief in knowing that you have a system that ensures bills are paid on time, without annoying late fees. The comfort you can take knowing that if something happens to you, your loved ones will be safe. The pride you have in having accumulated long-term security. The better organized you are about your finances, the less you have to think about money, the more time you have to live your life. And that's what it's all about.

And then there's the stuff . . .

Financial clutter always takes the form of paper. Let's dive into it.

Files

File cabinets are full of papers you will never look at again. I'm convinced that 80 percent of what goes into a filing cabinet never sees the light of day again. It's incredibly difficult to throw away files. After all, at some point in time you thought this piece of paper was so valuable that it deserved to be *filed*. And now you're going to just . . . throw it away? The answer is, *yes*. That's exactly what you're going to do—on a regular basis comb through your files and discard those once-indispensable, now completely unnecessary pieces of paper.

Tax stuff

I dealt a lot with paperwork and filing in *It's All Too Much: An Easy Plan for Living a Richer Life with Less Stuff*, but it's probably worth repeating here some of those broad and fairly conservative guidelines for managing your bills and financial records for tax season and audits. My official disclaimer is that you shouldn't take my word for it and should check with your own accountant or financial adviser to verify that this information is up-to-date and accurate for your state and situation.

Tax Trash Calendar

Every month:

- Toss out ATM, bank deposit slips, and credit card receipts after you have checked them against your bank or credit card statements.
- Toss out receipts for minor purchases, unless there is a warranty or refund involved.

Every year:

- Toss out your monthly bank and credit card statements (unless you require proof of deductions for taxation purposes)—most credit card companies provide a year-end summary that you can retain.
- Toss out monthly mortgage statements provided you receive a year-end summary of your account.
- Toss out pay stubs after they are checked against your W-2 or 1099.
- Toss out your W-2 and 1099 forms from seven years ago and earlier.
- Toss out canceled checks and receipts or annual statements for:
  - mortgage interest from seven years ago and earlier.
  - property taxes from seven years ago and earlier.
  - deductible business expenses or other tax-deductible expenses from seven years ago and earlier.

Keep indefinitely:

- Annual tax returns.
- Year-end summary statements from financial institutions.

- Receipts for the purchase of any investments you own.
- Receipts for home-improvement costs or major purchases that may be needed for insurance claims or similar.

If you want to check the official word on this, read what Uncle Sam has to say at the website of the Internal Revenue Service. Download Publication No. 552 at www.irs.gov for complete details of what to keep and what you can let go of to keep the tax man happy.

Unopened mail

Overstuffed files create stress and disorganization. That's bad enough. But unopened mail always creates money problems. Those sealed envelopes contain bills that increase as they go unpaid. They contain reminders of the deposit due to hold your child's place in school. They hold notices of changes in credit card rates. They hold insurance reimbursement checks that don't earn you interest until they're deposited. The longer you ignore envelopes, the more they build up. Unpaid bills get sent again so you have twice the work to figure out how much you owe. And the pile sits there, on the table in the entrance hall or, worse, spread across the dining room table, a constant reminder to you (and your family, if you have one) that life isn't secure. Things aren't under control. Disaster looms. Remember what I said at the beginning of this chapter? No more paperwork procrastination. That's where I wanted you to start and it's where I'll end. Start with the clutter. Clear it out, clarify your goals, and make the life

Dear Peter:

My number one nemesis is the mail. I've organized it, got all kinds of folders and bins and stackable organizers, put myself on the "do not mail" direct-mail list, hired two professional organizers, switched to online bill pay, and used countless "systems" to try to keep on top of the mail and bills. And it keeps coming. More and more of it.

Seems like no matter what I do, I still miss important mail. I get those embarrassing calls that I am late on a payment (and I have the money to pay the bill!). I was stopped at the airport because my license was expired—the renewal notice got put in the wrong pile. I even had the electric company come out to the house to cut off my electricity—because the automatic bill pay didn't go through and I missed all three notices. The mail pile is about a foot high today, and that's just from the last week (and, I already purged the obvious junk mail). What do I do about this?

you want a reality. Are you ready to go? Here's a quick cheat sheet for tackling your home office and financial clutter:

- Create a vision for the space where you handle your finances. There should be an inbox for bills to be paid and whatever supplies you need to pay them (computer or checkbook, envelopes, and stamps).
- Overcome obstacles that prevent you from doing paperwork. Come clean with yourself and your partner and prepare to move forward.

- Commit time, even if it's only twenty minutes during which you sort and shred every day. Just make sure you prioritize your current paperwork. Handle new papers first, then spend leftover time dealing with the old.
- Communicate with your partner about your shared vision for managing your finances. If you aren't both committed, you won't succeed.
- Set boundaries. Live within your means. If you tend to overspend, give yourself a twenty-four-hour cooling-off period before committing to a purchase.
- Make changes. Only by changing the role stuff plays in your life will you be able to stop buying more things, let go of the clutter, and find a financial balance that makes sense for the life you want.
- Live in the present, but set aside funds for the future as soon as a paycheck comes in so you can live with the confidence that you'll continue to enjoy life.
- Face fears. Owning up to your money troubles is the first step toward solving them. If you ignore debt, it gets worse fast.
- Celebrate successes. As you simplify your finances, you will feel more relaxed and secure. You work hard for your money. Enjoy knowing that you're making the most of it.

5

Health

The cluttered body

Phil was a busy television producer who ate whatever he wanted, went running once a week if he had time, and never otherwise exercised until he entered a push-up competition with the other guys in his office. A week later he was flat on his back with a herniated disk. He told me, "Fifteen years ago, I could have done fifty push-ups, no problem. But apparently I'm not twenty anymore." You live in your body. When you're healthy you barely notice the complex systems that enable you to grow, move, think, eat, and otherwise make the most of your life. But when your health fails you, life comes to a halt. A flu, a broken leg, an allergy attack—you have a million things to do, but when something goes wrong you have to stop and give your body the attention it demands.

Catching a virus may be out of your control, but keeping your body as healthy and strong as it can be is your responsibility. Do you feel at your best? When was the last time you had a physical? Does everyone in your family have a doctor? A dentist? Is your health insurance the best it can be? Are you in good physical shape? Do you make time to exercise? How is your mental health? Are you stressed? Anxious? Unhappy?

> Dear Peter:
> I took several days off from work to declutter. My wonderful husband and I tossed out a lot of trash. We have bags full of personal data to shred, but we threw out large trash bags of junk. We reclaimed a room with a closet and a huge storage closet. I cleaned out my side of the bedroom. Guess what???!!! I now have room to put down my exercise mat and I did thirty minutes of exercise in the morning!!! I did jumping jacks, push-ups, chest presses, triceps, biceps, sit-ups and a little yoga.

Good health is about more than being stylishly slender. Good health is mental and physical. It is waking up in the morning rejuvenated, ready to greet the day. It is feeling comfortable in your body and exuding confidence. Our bodies are complex and imperfect. Good health is knowing that you are giving yourself your best shot at living long and well. It sounds so fundamental. Who *wouldn't* want to be healthy? And yet often, when it comes to our health we are our own greatest obstacles. What gets in the way? Often the daily clutter of places to go, people to see, and things to do sidetracks us and we forget to prioritize our health. But sometimes the clutter is emotional. The clutter of fear, anger, loneliness, or denial obscures the path to health just as solidly as a pile of diet books stacked high on an unused treadmill. Have you stopped paying attention to your body? Is your relationship with your body cluttered by:

- Your emotional relationship with food?
- Stress that gets in the way of clear thinking?
- Mixed-up priorities that interfere with exercise?

Have you stopped making the most of the body you live in in the same way you gave up on your home, allowing clutter to overtake it? Does the clutter of everyday life distract you from taking care of yourself?

Quiz
Are You at Home in Your Body?

1. How do you feel when you wake up in the morning?
    a. I feel energized and ready to greet the day.
    b. I could sleep another couple of hours, but coffee should get me through the day.
    c. I want to pull the covers back over my head.

2. The adjective that best describes your daily state of mind is:
    a. Together. I'm pretty organized and on top of things.
    b. Scatterbrained. I do my best, but feel like I've got too many balls in the air.
    c. Exhausted. I'm just glad when I make it through the day.

3. When you look in the mirror, you feel:
    a. Satisfied. My body isn't perfect, but it matches who I am and how I feel inside.
    b. Disappointed. I can't believe that's me.
    c. Forget it. I avoid mirrors altogether.

4. When you think about how you treat your body (what you eat, how much you exercise, etc.):
   - a. *I feel proud. I work hard to be healthy.*
   - b. *I feel guilty. I know what needs to be done, but just can't seem to do it.*
   - c. *I hate myself. If I die young, I'll be the only one to blame.*

5. In the middle of the night:
   - a. *I'm dead asleep.*
   - b. *I sometimes wake up worried about work, family, etc.*
   - c. *I pop a sleeping pill—or feel like I should. I'm plagued by insomnia.*

6. If your children, parents, or loved ones approached their health the way you do:
   - a. *That would be fine.*
   - b. *I'd want them to make some changes.*
   - c. *I'd be seriously worried for them.*

7. Your chances of living to a ripe old age are:
   - a. *As good as anyone else's.*
   - b. *Anyone's guess.*
   - c. *Not very good if I keep going at this rate.*

Are you at home in your body?

If your answers are mostly As:
Even if you don't think you're 100 percent perfect, you seem to be living your life to the fullest. You have a good sense of

your own self-worth. You care about yourself, and you treat your body accordingly. Not only that, you decide what you want to do, and do it. You don't feel physically limited, or let self-consciousness about your appearance stand in your way.

If your answers are mostly Bs:
It's time to make some changes. You knew that answer was coming, and I'm guessing it's because you're unhappy with your body, but something gets in the way of your making real changes. Do you really want to go on like this for the rest of your life? It's time for you to love yourself as much as you love those around you. It's time for you to take control of your life once and for all. It's time for you to clear away the clutter of excuses and fear, listen to your own voice, to hear what you want, and to achieve it.

If your answers are mostly Cs:
Life is passing you by. You are missing out on the joys and adventures of life, limited by your body and mind. Unless you have a medical problem, you have the power to change all this. Either accept yourself or change yourself, but do not stand in the way of your own well-being.

Imagine the body you want

You may feel like *you*, your *self*, is your mind. Your mind, after all, is where all the thoughts and hopes and dreams and decisions of life take place. But your mind is stuck, for better or worse, in your body. It is your body that has to live out that life you so desire. So now I want you to think about what you want from your body. How does your body serve your life goals?

*What do you want **from** your body?*

Let me help you get started.

• Comfort

An unhealthy body is uncomfortable. Poor diet and/or lack of exercise leave you feeling tired and moody. Stress affects your blood pressure and cholesterol. A stressful job can exacerbate any existing health problems you have. In contrast, a healthy body is comfortable. Balanced, nutritious foods make you feel energized and even-keeled. Regular exercise improves your mood, reduces your risk of injury, and helps you sleep well. Plus, if you are eating and exercising well, you have the comfort of knowing you're taking good care of yourself.

Dear Peter:
I'm trying to reprioritize my daily routines and do some things for myself now. For instance, I've wanted to take a yoga class for some time now, but never felt right about spending money on myself (I could add silly rules like that to the list of clutter). Now, finally, I realize if I don't, I'm not going to last long as I'm quickly burning out. I guess the reasons don't really matter, but now that I'm clearing out the clutter, I need to work on finding some value in myself and stop putting myself last.

• Appearance

Every body is different, and if you aren't genetically predisposed, all the vegetables and Pilates in the world can't change you into a six-foot-tall size 0. But it's no great revelation that taking care of

your body improves your appearance. You can improve your appearance simply by decluttering your relationship with your body. A clear, simple, healthy approach to life will do wonders for your appearance. It's worth finding out how you feel and look after reaching that achievable goal. You might be surprised to find that once you are healthy, that intense need to be skinny fades away.

- **Physical ability**

Your body gets you places. Where do you want to go? Do you want to climb mountains? Do you want to play with your children or grandchildren without getting tired? Do you want to feel younger? Sit at your desk all day without getting stiff? What are the physical goals you have for your body?

- **Safety**

Part of being healthy is creating a safe, clean environment that fosters well-being. A clean, safe house nurtures you. Being prepared for emergencies gives you the peace of mind to sleep nights.

- **Longevity**

Lung cancer, heart disease, diabetes, osteoporosis—you can't entirely eliminate your chances of getting a disease, but you can certainly reduce them. Most of us would like to maximize our life expectancy, and to live for as long as possible in as strong a physical condition as possible. No matter when or how late you commit to living a healthier, longer life, you will see results.

Clear the clutter of unreal expectations

Superficial things first. I'm guessing that you aren't a supermodel and chances are that you're not going to be one. Not only that, you

Activity
Define Your Vision for a Healthy Body and a Healthy You

With a clearer sense of what you want from your ideal body, now fill in the chart below.

How do you feel about your health and body now?

What do you want from your body:

- In your 30s
- In your 40s
- In your 50s
- In your 60s
- Beyond your 60s

What do you need to change in order to achieve a healthy, strong body?

don't have a God-given right to be thin. All those products guaranteeing that, in some incredibly short amount of time and with no effort, you will have a stunning body are playing on your sense of entitlement. You think you deserve to be perfect, and that a magic cellulite-erasing, hair-growing, stomach-reducing, breast-lifting, muscle-building, butt-reducing, pain-and-suffering–free remedy is just around the corner. In the meantime, you can eat and drink whatever you want and only exercise your excuses. Wrong. Everyone is dealt a different set of body genes, and it does you no good to fight against the way you are born.

Being realistic means more than accepting who you are and who you might become. It also means taking responsibility for what you do with your body and what you put into it. Did you ever understand the expression, "You can't have your cake and eat it, too"? How about, "You can't eat your cake and lose weight, too"? When I declutter homes, I remind the residents that they are the ones who brought all that stuff into their living space. Unless your only clutter issue is junk mail, the clutter didn't arrive by itself and it won't go away on its own. The same is true for the extra pounds of fat on your body. You put them there. You ate more calories than you burned. It's a simple fact. No, weight isn't the only aspect of health. But cigarette smoking isn't exactly an exploding trend. America has a fat problem, but the problem isn't America's. It's yours. The life you are living and the choices you are making are making you fat. If you are overweight (serious medical issues aside), you are not taking good care of your body. Now is the time to step up to the plate, to take responsibility for who you are, and to do the work you must do to achieve your goals.

Skinny isn't the answer
Deep down, do you believe that if you lose weight all of your problems will be solved? You'll meet the man or woman of your

dreams. You'll get a better job. You'll be beautiful. You'll be *happy*. Not so. Thin doesn't guarantee happiness. Fat may manifest itself most obviously on our hips or midsections, but the real battlefield in weight loss is that space between our ears. It's important to face the issues that clutter our relationship with food and get ourselves to a healthy weight. It will improve how you feel and increase your chances at a long life. But meanwhile, don't postpone life.

Watch out for obstacles

Why is change so hard? You may tell yourself that there are obstacles in your way, and that these obstacles are out of your control. Sometimes, this is true. Your job is all-consuming. Your health is poor for reasons out of your control. Someone put that slab of chocolate cake on the table in front of you, dammit! But most of the obstacles that arise are excuses or challenges that you can and should overcome.

Not enough time

This is the excuse I hear more than any other. Exercise takes time. Doctors' appointments interrupt your day. Shopping for and preparing healthy meals is impossible. It's a pain to apply sunscreen. You don't have the opportunity or money to destress. You say you don't have the time, but what, I ask you, is taking precedence over your health and well-being? One principle that I hold firmly to is that we make time for what we value. The time exists, I promise you. Spend less time shopping for clothes to hide behind and more time out walking, as far from the TV as possible. Make salads for dinner—they require barely any prep time at all. If you're caring for young children, sneak in short bursts of exercise while they run around at the playground or nap. Bike to work. Pass on the elevator and walk a couple of flights of stairs. Get your cholesterol tested. Find the time now and you won't spend it in doctors' offices later trying to fix the damage of years of unhealthy living.

Cluttered priorities

You may have the best intentions, but when life overwhelms you and you're busy with work, family, or both, is your health the first thing you sacrifice? I know a husband and wife who are in couples' therapy, but one of the partners misses their session week after week. How is that *couples'* therapy? If your marriage is suffering enough that you are in therapy, yet you can't make it to a session, what message are you sending to your partner about your marriage? For many of us, when we're tired or overrun, exercise is the first thing to go. When life gets busy, fast food seems like the easiest option. Of course, none of us is perfect, but once you've allowed your health to slide down the ladder of priorities, you'll find that it has a tendency to stay where it has landed. Your work clears up, but you're out of the habit of going to the gym and in the habit of eating fast food. Or, what is more likely the case, your work pace never eases up. You never make it to therapy. Or the gym. Or the grocery store. You never get that odd freckle examined by a dermatologist. Your car gets so dirty that you can barely see out the window when you drive. All these decisions are risks to your health, and if you keep taking those risks, you will regret it one day. Mark my words.

Cluttered history

Some of us were raised in households where taking care of your body just wasn't an issue. Maybe the food you ate wasn't the healthiest or your family believed that going to the doctor was a sign of weakness. Or maybe your family paid so much attention to what you ate and how you looked that your laissez-faire attitude is a form of rebellion. In either case, it's time you left the clutter of your past behind. The choices that you make for your health should be based on the body you want to have and the life you want to live in that body. You need to shift from making emotional decisions to making intellectual decisions. It's hard to shift your mentality from what you grew up believing was normal. It's easier said than done, but I'm going to get you started.

Fear of bad news

A new patient walks into a dentist's office. The man is attractive and nicely dressed, but when the dentist looks into his mouth he sees inflamed gums and rotting teeth. "How long has it been since you've seen a dentist? Things don't look good in here." The man says, "I was afraid you'd say that. That's why I didn't want to come." How many dentists do you think can tell this story or a similar one? My guess is 100 percent. The moral here is obvious. Being in denial makes things worse. It is important to take stock of your body and to be responsible for it.

No monitoring

Is willpower your issue? If you are having trouble reaching your goals, it always helps to keep track of your efforts. Be it an exercise log or a food journal, the best way to guarantee that you are honoring your commitment to yourself is to hold yourself to it on paper, to be honest with yourself when you stray, and to return to the plan with renewed vigor.

Activity
What's Getting in the Way of My Ideal Health?

Reviewing the sections above, write down the obstacles that stand in your way of achieving the state of health you'd like.

• _____

• _____

• _____

Declutter your health

Commit time

For many people, the concept of health has become fused with the concept of medical care. In this way of thinking, health comes from a doctor, a particular drug, or a course of treatment. Obviously, the medical profession has a role to play, but their focus is very much on treatment, not on the promotion of good health. By the time you get to a doctor, chances are something is wrong. There are lots of things each of us can do to increase our chances of staying out of the doctor's office and keeping healthy.

Your health is determined by your lifestyle (except when genetics or accidents or bad luck come to play, but those health issues are best handled by the experts). There is nothing harder than changing the way you behave on a daily basis. Why? Because you got yourself there. No matter how passive your approach to life is, over time you made a series of decisions that add up to how you now spend the hours in your day. This didn't happen overnight, and it's not going to change overnight. Think of the hours in your day the way I do—as a house cluttered with years of failed hobbies and ill-fitting clothes. You can't snap your fingers and wish the clutter away. You need to clear it away item by item, making small (and often hard) decisions and breaking poor habits. Change comes with choice and each decision you make moves you either closer to a healthier life or further from it.

Time to assess your health and treat problems
Think about all the time you invest in maintaining your car or your home. You don't miss an oil change, but when was the last time you got a checkup? If you have children, do you take them to the doctor regularly and maintain health records for them? What makes you think you don't need the same attention? Did you know that adults need booster shots and new immunizations? When was the last time you saw your doctor? In a general examination, a doctor can identify early markers for serious problems.

Time to move
Like it or not, you need to move that body. If you're not a fan of exercise (and most people aren't), then don't think of it as exercise, think of it instead as time set aside exclusively for you, time dedicated to the new and improved you. It's about moving more and moving to the place you want to be.

Moving (or exercise!) takes time. Increasing your heart rate on a regular basis provides significant benefits to your body, especially your cardiovascular system. Lifting weights increases muscle mass, which in turn burns more calories. It also helps prevent bone disease. But weight lifting takes time as you work your way slowly through the muscle groups. Stretching, which increases flexibility, balance, and coordination and releases stress, also takes time (the longer you do it, the better it feels).

Increase the time you commit to exercise gradually. If you don't exercise already, start by incorporating more activity into your daily life. Walk instead of driving. Take stairs instead of elevators. If you spend time working at a desk or watching TV, incorporate short breaks for physical activity. (Keep it appropriate to your workplace, of course. I'm not suggesting leg lifts in the middle of a busy office.)

Next, step it up by committing to a regular activity that you enjoy (or, if you don't like exercising at all, the activity that is least unbearable). Start a yoga class, get a bike, walk the dogs, buy a workout VHS or DVD, join a stroller workout class, play tennis with your family, start an ultimate Frisbee league. Whatever it is, start by doing it for half an hour at least, three times a week.

Finally, balance your exercise regimen and increase your time commitment by including cardiovascular activity, weight lifting, and stretching. I'll talk about how later in "Make Changes."

Time to eat healthy food
Eating well takes time because it requires planning. If you leave your meal decisions till the moment when you're walking into your home after a long day at work, you'll inevitably choose what's easiest or most convenient, not what's best for you. Without planning, the easy choice is always the first choice. Being organized, on the other hand, makes the good choice the easy choice. When you don't plan, you wind up eating poorly, running into a fast-food restaurant or wolfing down junk food. Don't let the time requirement of being organized dissuade you from eating well, because eating poorly consumes time in a different way: It makes you fat, which means you have to spend more time working out in an effort to lose the weight. It also makes you unhealthy, which means

you have to spend time—and suffer!—with whatever ailments result. Even dieting wastes time because dieting is temporary planning. You think you can lose weight and then return to your same old bad habits. Well, it isn't news to anyone who has tried them that diets don't work—forty-five million Americans a year learn this the hard way! Going on and off diets takes much more time and leads to disappointment and failure. Instead, if you get in the habit of planning your meals, you will develop healthy habits that last you the rest of your life. A time commitment? Yes. A waste of time? I think not.

Time to maintain

Think about all you do to maintain your home. You fix small leaks before they become big leaks and cause water damage. If you own your home, you maintain your heat and air-conditioning systems. If you live in a house, you clean the rain gutters. If a toilet overflows, you unstop it, but you may also try to understand what caused the problem in the first place so that it doesn't stop up again. And (I hope) you clean your house on a regular basis, vacuuming dust, mopping floors, wiping counters, scrubbing bathrooms, etc. You do all of this for two reasons: 1) to prevent large problems from occurring, and 2) to increase your enjoyment of your home.

It should be the same with your health. Stop and think for a moment: What do you do on a regular basis to promote and sustain your good health? If you're struggling to find an answer, what does that tell you about your commitment to yourself? Wanting to avoid illness is a reasonable thing, but a far better goal is to feel energized, focused, motivated, and healthy every day.

Activity
Health Maintenance Checklist

You know how to maintain your house. How do you go about maintaining your health?

- Know your health insurance plan and maximize its benefits.
- See a general practitioner, gynecologist, dentist, eye doctor, and any relevant specialists for regular checkups.
- Be proactive about any problems or chronic issues.
- Seek help for mental health issues, including marital problems.
- Keep your home clean and safe.
- Have emergency supplies at home, at work, and in any cars you own.
- Stay on top of the health care needs of your children and/or aging parents.
- Attend to the health needs of any pets you own.

Communicate

I'm confident that most people in this country know how to be healthy. How to eat healthy food. How to exercise. Why stress is bad. When to see a doctor. In each of us, there is a roadblock or hurdle that stands between what we know we should do and what we actually do. Knowing what's right isn't the issue. Doing it is the problem. We ignore the internal voice saying, "Don't eat that cheesecake! It's bad for you!" So instead of telling you what you've heard before, I want to help you teach yourself to listen to that inner voice.

Find allies to help you achieve your goals. Transform unhealthy traditions into new habits that make you a stronger, healthier person. Do you and your best friend love to go out for ice cream together? Can you take up walking or yoga instead? If your boss is intolerant of your efforts to take care of a sick family member, can you talk to someone in Human Resources? Will a colleague join you on the walk to work? Can you exercise with fellow stay-at-home moms? If you have chronic health problems, can you join an online group of people dealing with the same issue?

Set boundaries

Health is the big picture
You've heard me say before that your home, your head, your heart, and your hips are intimately connected. In fact, the more work I do with families and their clutter, the more I see the connectedness of the different facets of our lives. How you perform at work. How you relate to the people you love. How you keep your house. How you feel about yourself. How much energy you have. How often you get sick. What you put in your body. Being cluttered throws you off balance. Just as going to sleep in a bedroom full of toys throws your sex life off balance, so a cluttered relationship with your body throws your health off balance.

If you collect too much of anything, including fat, you can't get rid of it without addressing the underlying issues. The same is true if you exercise too little or too much, or pay too little or too much attention to your physical state. What are the issues that stand in your way? Are you stuck living an unhealthy lifestyle that you inherited from your parents? Are you too self-conscious to exercise? Do you think of yourself as someone who hates exercise in any form? Do you eat food when you're not hungry? To achieve the body and look you desire, you have to consider the life you want to live. You have to look at your body the way you look at your house and say, "Do I honor and respect this body? Does it reflect who I am?" If your goals aren't clear and your thinking isn't focused, you can't break the habits and clear the clutter that stands in your way.

Create space for good habits

Are you an active or passive participant in your own life? One of the most common ways we fail to treat ourselves well is to do little. It's easy to treat yourself poorly. Spending hours in front of the TV every night is passive. It doesn't *feel* like you're doing anything harmful, but inactivity is bad for you, especially because it's so insidious. And then there's the food. Our world is absolutely full of delicious foods. Unfortunately, many of those delicious foods are absolutely full of chemicals, fat, and sugar. The surest way to improve your health forever is bringing good, wholesome, home-cooked meals into your life. If you're not in the habit of preparing balanced and varied meals of fish, vegetables, and complex carbohydrates, you need to deliberately set aside time and energy to do so. You are worth the investment and it will return huge dividends.

When we believe something to be important we invest of ourselves in it. What's important becomes a priority and a focus for us. Stop for a moment and think about this: If health is not a priority for you, if you constantly make the easy choice rather than the good one, what does that say about what you value? When you make yourself a priority, then habits that contribute to a better you become an important part of every day. I want you to focus on what you want from your body and your life. It's about the setting, the company, and the spirit with which you live every day. Don't run mindlessly on a treadmill, unless that brings you pleasure. Make activity a fulfilling part of your life. Don't shovel down tasteless food in front of the TV. Find recipes that make meals delicious, healthy, and exciting.

What I'm trying to show you is that you can replace the cheap thrill of instant gratification by giving your body a deeper value, both psychically and nutritionally. Further, I believe that when you make this commitment to yourself, others will begin to do the same. Value yourself first and those around you will follow suit.

Don't overcommit

I'm all for sudden, dramatic changes, but let's be realistic. If you try to transform yourself overnight from being a junk-food junkie/ couch potato to being a health nut/exercise freak how likely are you to stick to your new regimen? Instead, I want you to set boundaries by making changes that you know you can commit to over the long haul. First, find room for exercise in your life. Then, as you get used to the activity, increase the intensity. Add new forms of exercise. The same goes for committing to a healthy diet. Make one change—like eliminating soda or white bread—and stick to it until it no longer feels like a major sacrifice. Then make another change. This measured approach is not only easier to practice, but it teaches you that improving your health isn't something you do once. It's something you work on until you die. I know one feisty ninety-six-year-old, Phyllis, who was told by her doctor that she no longer had to worry about her cholesterol. He said, "Congratulations. You did it. You've had low cholesterol for decades, and now you don't have to worry about clogging your arteries. You can eat as much red meat as you want." I asked Phyllis if she was going to go out and have a big steak, but she said, "Oh, no. Watching my cholesterol has gotten me this far. I'm not about to stop." Good health is not just about what you eat or what you do, it's about how you live.

Is your job making you sick?

A stressful job can take over your life. If it's impacting your health, it has to be changed. I know that's a radical statement. You're in this job for a reason, and most jobs come with some level of stress. But look at it from the other side. Is this job really worth what it's costing you? I'm not saying you have to quit, but you can affect your blood pressure and cholesterol simply by making changes in how you approach the stress of your job.

What you buy is what you eat

I tell my clients, "If you don't have room in your house, you shouldn't buy more stuff." When it comes to food, you shouldn't buy the foods that make you fat. Period. If you want to allow yourself a treat, don't buy a big bag of cookies and tell yourself you'll only have one cookie. We both know that isn't true and never will be. Sure, cheese is good for you. But if you can't have cheese in the house without eating a brick at a time then, you guessed it, you can't have cheese in the house. It's okay to experiment with buying foods that are already divided into portion sizes (like single-serving sticks of mozzarella). If the experiment fails—sorry, no more cheese. Everything counts. It doesn't matter if someone hands you a bag of chips as a free sample, it still counts. Even if you eat dessert at a restaurant or an office party, it still counts. Just because you exercise right before you buy an ice-cream cone, the cone still counts. Food you eat off someone else's plate, including your children's, still counts. Food you sneak in the privacy of your car at the drive-thru on the way home still counts. No more games or lying to your food journal and yourself. No matter how quickly they go down or how good they taste, those foods are real, and so are the consequences to your body.

Make changes

Clean your unhealthy home

Nobody can live a healthy life in a cluttered home—it's just not possible. I've seen firsthand the havoc that a cluttered, messy, disorganized mess can wreak on a family. Where there's clutter, there are almost always health problems of different kinds. The dust and grime buildup greatly contribute to respiratory problems. Mold is really common in rooms where air can't circulate because of the volume of stuff filling a space. If there are animals in the house, the problem is even further compounded. And those are just the physical health issues. Clutter causes stress and anxiety, loss of focus, a sense of powerlessness, and often social isolation that can be debilitating. At its worst, the clutter can even kill. Just a couple of years ago, a woman who was reported missing in a Pacific Northwest town was found dead in her own home sometime later. The woman had suffocated after a pile of clutter and debris had collapsed on her. Clutter sucks the life out of homes and lives in ways most people don't even think about.

Even if your home isn't cluttered, attend to its cleanliness. Is your bed clean and made? What's underneath it? When was the last time you cleaned under your refrigerator? Do you regularly change the filters on your heater and scrub the mold and mildew from your shower and bathtub?

Make a safe home

The whole point of being healthy is living a long life with as few health issues as possible. It stands to reason that you should take all steps you can to avoid catastrophe. This means making sure your home is equipped with smoke and carbon monoxide detectors. You should have fire extinguishers readily accessible on each floor, especially in the kitchen. Make sure your kitchen fire extinguisher is approved for grease fires. Some of the newer fire extinguishers have a button you can press to check the pressure. Do so once a month. When a smoke alarm battery dies, replace it immediately instead of taking the battery out and forgetting about it.

Keep emergency supplies, including plenty of water, in your home and office. Check these supplies once a year to make sure their contents haven't gone out of date. Make a plan so that the entire family knows where to go and who to call in an emergency. Redcross.org sells emergency and first aid kits and offers guidance for how to prepare for the unexpected.

Drive a safe car
Drive safely. We all know that driving is one of the most dangerous things we do, and yet every day I see people weaving dangerously through traffic in hope of making it home, what—five minutes sooner? We're all eager to see our families, but it's not worth putting yourself and others in danger. When buying a car, put safety ratings first. I shouldn't have to tell you that it's never worth drinking and driving. Your reflexes are compromised long before you know them to be. Be wary of other drivers, particularly on holidays. Keep your car clean. Are there old juice boxes and rotting food bits hiding away in the backseat? What's growing back there? Be sure to keep your car well-maintained. When your car breaks down, you not only incur costs, but, more critically, you risk an accident. Old tires are dangerous, and you should always have a reliable spare. Stock your car with emergency supplies like a first aid kit, flares, a blanket, walking shoes (if you wear heels), and an emergency kit with food, water, and survival gear.

Keep your children in rear-facing car seats for as long as they meet the weight requirements. Facing backward is the safest position in an accident. For older children, invest in a booster seat. Follow all installation instructions to the tee. If you have any doubts, have a professional check the seat for you (see www.seat check.org).

Declutter your health records

Imagine if something like a car accident put you out of commission, and you were unable to communicate. Are your health records in order? Would someone be able to see who to contact, what health conditions you have, when your last checkup occurred, etc.? Your health records should be up to date regardless. Do you have an internist, a dentist, a gynecologist, and (if relevant) a pediatrician that you know by name and can call with questions?

If you have a chronic problem—asthma, allergies, high blood pressure, etc.—make sure all your medicine and health insurance information is up to date. With the new higher deductibles, do you have the best plan for lifelong medication? Keep yourself involved in treatment developments. New medications and procedures emerge constantly, and there's no guarantee that your doctor is doing his research.

If you're responsible for the health care of older parents or your children, you need to be responsible about getting them to regular appointments, making sure they follow the doctor's advice, and keeping well-organized records.

Don't let your physical ailments become the clutter that you hide behind. Some people resist treatment because having a physical problem allows them to feel excused from certain activities or responsibilities in life. When the issues run this deep, it can be hard to overcome them and seek help, or to persuade an ailing loved one to do so. But nobody should live with chronic pain if it can be avoided. If you focus on this truth, it alone should be enough to motivate you or a loved one out of the depression or apathy that imprisons you.

If you have pets, you're responsible for their health records, too. Do they have all their shots? Are they flea-free and safe from rabies? Do you bathe them regularly? Are your house and car (relatively) free from pet hair? Please don't be one of those people whose animals make mistakes in the house. It is just intolerable. If you can't train your pet, find someone who can.

ICE your cell phone

I'm not suggesting storing your cell phone in the freezer, but rather making sure that if you're incapacitated or in an accident that those assisting you can quickly and efficiently contact your loved ones.

ICE is an acronym for In Case of Emergency. Enter the word "ICE" into your cell phone in the same way you'd enter any new contact name and then enter the numbers you'd want called in an emergency. First responders and emergency workers will check for these numbers and know exactly whom to call.

Insurance

Insurance is the bet that you hedge against health issues. It's tough to stomach, because it's expensive, and the payout only comes when something goes wrong, so it's never a gamble that has a happy payday. Nonetheless, it is protection that we all need.

Health insurance is critical to surviving our medical system. The better you understand it, the more you can do to maximize its benefits. Make sure you know if certain doctors will cost you less. If you are hospitalized unexpectedly, when and how does your insurance company need to be informed? What kind of coverage is available for your family? Are there additional benefits like gym reimbursement, mental heath coverage, and flexible spending plans that can help you cover health-related expenses? Refamiliarize yourself with your plan and its options every year. Plans change and so do your needs.

Your employer may include disability insurance as part of your benefits package, but it may not be enough to carry your family if something happens to you. If you are self-employed, you will need to purchase disability insurance independently.

Life insurance is also part of most companies' benefits packages. One easy way to think about how much life insurance you need is—at minimum—to make sure your partner could pay off your remaining mortgage or purchase a home. From there, look at how much your partner earns and how much additional income he or she would need to continue living at your current level. Losing you would be hard enough. Your partner doesn't need financial troubles on top of that.

The clutter of stress and mental health

I've talked about stress as the catch-all term that we employ when life just seems unmanageable. In the same way that lots of little things accumulate to clutter a home, too many demands coming from too many different directions stress us out. Stress descends on single people trying to juggle high-pressure careers, and on parents trying to balance work, soccer practice, ballet classes, grocery shopping, homework help, food preparation, and marriage. Do you feel pressured to be an überparent, arranging playdates when there isn't time, shuttling your child to six birthday parties every weekend, volunteering to chaperone trips when it conflicts with your job?

When you come home from work, do you walk into a house that is loud or quiet? Are you assaulted with demands? Do you drop your bag and start cooking dinner? Are there children to be fed, helped with homework, and bathed?

How do you deal with job stress? Do you reward yourself by shopping or eating? ("I work hard, I deserve these shoes.") During your lunch hour, are you able to relax, or do you wolf down fast food at your desk, then grab a candy bar or donut to get yourself over the afternoon hump every day? Is there anything you do to unwind during the day at work or is every conversation at work about how crappy work is?

All this adds to the confusion of life. You're overcommitted, wanting to please everyone, trying to be perfect. You don't know what a week holds until you study the calendar. When you're operating at such high speed, you don't have time to slow down or talk. Communication suffers in all areas of your life. Trying to do everything takes its toll—it gets harder to do things *mindfully*.

If you're overtaxed, you're constantly depleted. All of this stress is clutter that gets in the way of mental and physical health. Emotionally, being overtaxed makes you exhausted, anxious, and angry. You feel out of control and instead of making calm, cool decisions that reflect your values and priorities, you opt for easy solutions in a desperate grab for anything that might bring relief. This means you might lash out at loved ones and feel unable to take pleasure in the joys of life. You might eat emotionally, oversleep, and obsess over situations without resolving anything. Physically, chronic stress has been linked to heart disease. Stress is associated with the development of high blood pressure, diabetes, a weakened immune system, and weight gain.

Finding stress relief
My recommendation for managing stress is a three-step approach. The first element is to find ways to physically decompress. Yoga, long walks, getting a massage, listening to music, bubble baths—try out different physical activities to find the ones that best allow your body to release pent-up energy.

When your body is relaxed, it's easier to think clearly. The next step is to sort out what is going on in your head.

Once you've gotten some perspective on your stress, it's time for step three—to focus on restructuring your life to make it less stressful. This is easier said than done. You can't change your job

Activity
Think Through Your Stress

Take some quiet time to reflect on when you are most stressed, where this stress originates, and how you respond to it. When you have some clear ideas, complete the following table.

What is the source of your stress?

How does your stress level affect you?
    Emotionally

    Physically

How does it affect those around you?

What are you doing to make your situation worse?

What changes can you make to your actions to relieve stress?

What changes can you make to your attitude to relieve stress?

What changes can you make to your surroundings to relieve stress?

or ditch family responsibilities overnight. But what you can do is establish some basic requirements for your life. Identify your primary needs and promise yourself that they will be met. This guarantees that one component of your life—whatever it is that's causing you stress—won't overwhelm everything else.

Back to basics
Food, sleep, exercise, fun, and space for decompression: these are the minimum needs that you owe it to yourself to preserve. If work or family responsibilities are getting in the way of any of these fundamental needs, you need to create space for them.

Food. Your life should allow you to eat nutritious food. You shouldn't have to hurry through your meal, and—though this may not be realistic for every meal of the day—you should take the time to savor your food and enjoy good company. See more about how to eat in "Eating for Health."

Sleep. Adults need seven to nine hours of sleep every night. You must find this time. Just because you've gotten away with less sleep doesn't mean that you don't need more. If you're a night owl who gets awakened by children at the crack of dawn, try going to bed earlier. Give it time. Think of yourself as a child who needs sleep training! If that doesn't work, see if you can work a nap into your schedule. *TIME* magazine reports that in-office napping is a "small but growing movement in corporate America to address the consequences of a nation of sleep-deprived workers."

Exercise. For healthy adults age eighteen to sixty-five, the American Heart Association and the American College of Sports Medicine recommend thirty minutes of moderate cardiovascular activity (like brisk walking) five times a week, or twenty minutes of vigorous activity (like running) three times a week. Additionally, they recommend muscle-strengthening activity twice a week. This is a *minimum*. The more the better. Being overweight is a major burden on your body, so if this amount of exercise isn't keeping your weight under control, you need to exercise more and address your diet. (See "Exercising for Health" for more information.)

Fun. Nothing counteracts stress better than laughter and joy. Fun doesn't always knock on your door and announce itself. You have to actively create space for it. Make plans to meet up with friends. Pursue hobbies. Create special moments with your partner and/ or your family. This is what life is truly made of. If you're stuck in a rut, consider the saying that a rut is just a coffin with the ends kicked out. Ouch! Maybe it's time to mix it up a little.

Space for decompression. Think about how you behave when you walk in the door after work. What is the first thing you do? Do you check your e-mail or voicemail messages? Do you hug your kids and say hello? Do you find a quiet place and take five minutes to recharge? Or grab a beer or glass of wine or bag of chips? If your life is busy, finding five minutes to yourself at key moments throughout the day can work wonders. Also, as a clutter expert, I must remind you that it is impossible to relax if your surroundings are cluttered. Be sure that your home and workspace are conducive to serenity. If you're not getting a sense of peace and calm, focus and motivation from your own home, where are you getting it from?

Exercising for health
Remember that exercise is not just a weight issue. Exercise now keeps you out of the doctor's office later. Exercise reduces your

risk for all the big health issues: heart disease, cancer, high blood pressure, and diabetes. It increases "good" cholesterol (HDL). It helps control weight and boosts self-esteem. As you get older, exercise is important in promoting bone strength, joint health, and good balance. So you're not off the hook if you're skinny by nature.

Don't tell me you hate exercise. Exercise is physical activity. It's moving your body. It's natural. If moving your body doesn't feel good, that's a real sign that something has to change. Now, if you're telling me you hate softball or spin classes, fine—me, too! Just as I'm not asking you to eat cardboard food, there's no need to participate in activities you don't like. What do you like? Walking with friends or your dog? Dancing? Swimming? Look for activities that are so pleasurable you forget they're also good for you.

Don't let your failed efforts at exercise become clutter. If that hideous treadmill sits unused in your basement, either start using it or get rid of it. Do you have a health club membership that you never use? Why not? Can you join a class there and commit to going once a week? If you can't make it to the gym, don't let that be your excuse for not exercising at all. Do leg lifts in front of the TV. Take a thirty-minute walk before work each day. If you can walk to a restaurant, volunteer to pick up lunch for colleagues at work. Run up and down the stairs in your home instead of piling things at the bottom or top of the staircase to wait for your next trip. I know a senior citizen who wears an iPod and paces the balcony of her apartment when it's too late for her to take a walk on the street. You can be a more active person throughout the day if you set your mind to it.

Eating for health

Diets are not about food, they're about decisions. The decisions that you make every day add up to the end results you live with. As with any change you want to make in your life, doing it occasionally, in brief spurts, never works. Clean your house once and before long the clutter will return with a vengeance. Diet temporarily and the fat will return. Exercise sporadically and you'll never feel stronger and will risk injuring yourself. You need to make realistic changes. Changes that build on one another. Changes that will last. Changes that make sense for who you are and what life you want to lead. This is not some new routine or regimen that you go "on" or "off," this is the way you choose to live your life.

> Dear Peter:
> I lost one hundred pounds last year. And, of course, the first thing I did before starting my diet, was to completely clean out all my kitchen cupboards and my fridge. I made a rule that only food "invited" into my home would go into my kitchen. I have kept it up and am maintaining my weight loss. Now I need to work on the rest of the house and on the rest of my issues.

We all have triggers—some emotional and some physical—that compel us to overeat. When you make a mistake, instead of hating yourself and deciding you'll never manage your diet, see it as an opportunity to gain some insight into your own behavior. Try keeping a food journal. Was it a certain time, place, or activity that triggered your lapse? Was it an emotional situation—celebration, frustration, loneliness? I don't want you to avoid holiday parties or

never to venture into your supermarket again because the candy aisle has obscene power over you. Instead, I want you to deliberately create new habits that help you dismantle the old ones. Small changes yield huge results. If there is a time of day when you overindulge, plan a tasty, healthy snack for exactly that time. If there is a place or event that is your weakness, prepare a meal for yourself to eat beforehand so you don't arrive with an appetite. If there's a special kind of food you can't resist, like sweets, find a healthy substitution, like sweet fruit, that you have at the ready to overcome a craving. If you have a fast-food habit, you're in the habit of getting food on the run and eating it on the run. The only way to change that habit is to plan, plan, plan.

Finding healthy food that you like to eat isn't hard. Your challenge is to summon the motivation, commitment, and ability to plan to eat the foods that are best for you. Food that you prepare at home will be healthier than anything you order in a restaurant. Ever wonder why restaurant food tastes so good? I have one word for you: butter. If you think restaurants care about your waistline, think again. All they want is for you to return to spend more money on yummy food. This doesn't mean you shouldn't enjoy eating out—if and when you truly enjoy it—but I want you to eat healthy meals at home. Prepare food on the weekend and freeze it. Do prep in the morning. Ask for help from your family. Choose meals where only one of the dishes requires real preparation, then steam vegetables and boil brown rice for quick-and-easy side dishes. Get simple recipes on the Web, in magazines, or from friends.

Make food choices based on priorities
When it comes to your diet, I want you to start making food choices based on your priorities. So start by asking yourself this question:

What do I want from my meals?

We're all in such a rush to wolf down our food that we forget to enjoy not only the food itself, but the experience of eating it. So really think about the question. What do you want from your meals?

- If all you want is to stop feeling hungry, regardless of what it does to your belly or thighs, go ahead, dive into those French fries or microwavable burrito bites!
- If your health and weight are more important than instant gratification, then you need to think about what you are eating.
- If you want to enjoy your food, to take pleasure in the meal, and to revel in the joy of a shared meal with loved ones, then you need to think about the total experience. Where you are sitting, what the table looks like, how the room is lit, and even what music is playing. You need to slow down, to taste each bite in your mouth, and to savor the conversation as you savor the meal.

I believe you're perfectly capable of designing your own healthy menu. And if you design it yourself, with the healthy foods that you actually enjoy, then you are developing new habits that are the basis for a lifetime of healthy eating. The more you are invested in the planning, the more likely you are to stick to it. It's simple: your plan, your meals, your life.

Live in the present

How many times have you promised yourself that you'll try harder . . . starting next week or after the next business trip, or after that party you have to go to over the weekend? You may be pretty committed to next week and to all the changes you're going to make then, but I'll tell you something—next week never arrives. This is your life. This minute. This hour. This day. If you push your plans into the future, you'll never get there. Those plans begin today and *lead* into the future. Yes, aspiration is good. You should always have your goals in mind. But the only way to achieve those goals is to see and be where you are. I want you to feel relaxed and safe in your home. I want you to be knowledgeable about your health status. I want you to eat foods for the body you want today. I want you to exercise today so you sleep well tonight. Every decision you make must support your commitment to the life you want here and now. Deal with the immediate and let next week take care of itself.

Don't just survive. Enjoy.
Be present in the moment. That means being aware of who you are, where you are, who you're with, what you're eating, and how it all fits into the life you want for yourself. I want you to find a calm awareness. When you sit down at the table, stop. Take a breath. Appreciate the moment, enjoy the people you're with, savor your food, walk while appreciating the world around you. The opportunity to talk and laugh and interact with your family and friends is as important as the steps you're taking toward a healthy body. It's around the table that much of the clutter of misunderstanding, of poor communication, of misplaced priorities can be addressed, resolved, and cleared out. Good health is about nourishing both your body and your soul.

Mindful indulgence
What's the point of having a beautiful and organized home, a perfect diet, and a perfect body if you don't take part in the art, culture, beauty, activity, and people of this world? Making your body

your temple isn't the be-all and end-all. You have to venture out of your safe haven and into the real world. Don't restrict yourself too rigidly. Instead, be aware. Remember who you are and who you want to be. If you're happy, you'll lose weight. Be happy. Enjoy the occasion. Gravitate to the life you want, seeking balance in all things.

Celebrate successes

The changes you make to your relationship, your job, and your family may make you happier, but they're hard to quantify. Even some of the changes you make to your financial landscape don't pay off until your twilight years. But if you clear the clutter of poor food choices, if you make changes toward a healthier life, you'll start feeling differently almost immediately. You'll feel energized. You'll sleep better. You'll take pride in the changes to your appearance. You may find it easier to fit into your clothes or that it's necessary to buy new, smaller clothes. Now, I hope I don't have to tell you that celebrating by wolfing down a pound of cheesecake is counterproductive. Remember that the goal is feeling better and being healthy. If you lose weight, being thinner will not make your problems magically disappear. You will have to deal with the clutter of your fat and the clutter that made you fat before you can be happy. Celebrate by taking pleasure in your new, healthy self as you progress toward having the body you want in the life you desire. Celebrate by enjoying a range of experiences and activities with the people you love.

And then there's the stuff . . .

- Create a vision of your healthy life. I've talked about how a cluttered house causes physical health problems, and I've talked about needing space to decompress. Think of it this way: You need space to move, work, eat, and live—step outside yourself and imagine what that space should look like. Now clear away everything that stands in the way of your health.

- Overcome obstacles. Don't let exercise gizmos, diet books, or unused health club memberships stand in your way. If you don't use it, get rid of it. Don't let fear or self-doubt prevent you from achieving the healthiest body you can have. Keep clear health records and practice preventative health care, visiting doctors for regular checkups.

- Commit time to clearing space in your home to prepare and eat healthy meals. The kitchen is holy ground. It's the place in your home that is vital to the sustenance of your family. The counters should be clear so you can prepare food in a clean, healthy environment. The shelves should be neat so you can find what you need. The refrigerator and pantry should be uncluttered so good, healthy, and nutritious food is readily accessible and doesn't go bad.

- Set boundaries. If you eat in front of the TV, you will eat greater quantities of food with less enjoyment. It will be harder for you to get your kids to eat the right foods in the right quantities. Don't do it. Your dining table reflects your attitude toward your meal. The space where you eat should be completely clear of everything except the food you are eating.

- Make changes. The practices you implement to maintain good health should be ongoing. Your house needs to be clean, safe, and well-maintained, and so does your body.

- Live in the present. This is the body you have for the rest of your life. Take active care of it and treat it with respect. Discard medicines that are out of date and any other products that you no longer need or use. Wash the shoes you wear to exercise. Get rid of clothes that don't fit.

- Face fears. Decluttering your relationship to your body may mean facing issues you never dealt with. Use what you learn to make changes. It will be hard, but uncovering hidden issues always leads to greater happiness. Seek professional help if you need it.
- Celebrate successes. A clean, safe home is a great foundation for a happy body and soul.

6

Our Sense of Well-Being

What's so difficult about peace, love, and understanding?

Language is powerful. We use it to convey our deepest emotions, to express our most intimate thoughts and strongest desires. The language of clutter is also incredibly powerful. When we speak of clutter, we conjure up very specific images. "I walked into that room and there was so much stuff, I couldn't breathe," or "The house is so full you feel like you are drowning," or "I feel suffocated in this space," or, most telling of all, "I feel buried in my own home." These are carefully chosen and laser-focused words. Somewhere in our souls, we know that clutter is stealing our lives. It sucks the life force from us and leaves us exhausted and with a sense of being drained and paralyzed.

The stuff you own can very easily separate you from the life you want—I've seen it happen in hundreds of homes in hundreds of different ways. We surround ourselves with things large and small, things that are intended to bring us joy and pleasure, things we like and often treasure. This is what we own, what we have, but what is it that we *want*? What is it that we are hoping for when we fill our homes with stuff?

> Dear Peter:
> Although I do not own a lot of "stuff," I use decluttering the material world as a diversion from dealing with my mental clutter. I would love to be able to declutter my mind. I want to begin defining my goals and take some steps in achieving them, but my mind is chaotic with the expectations and old messages of others, and I lack clarity. I want my mental space to have creativity, joy, and peace.

I've talked about clearing the clutter in your relationships and your family, in your work and finances, and in your health. These are all areas of your life where you need to function in a context. You strive to have a mutually rewarding relationship with your loved ones, you try to be successful and fulfilled in your work, and you aim to bring healthy food and exercise to your body. But what about when you put all those things aside? Who are you when you are alone in the dark? How do you feel inside when you float in the swimming pool of life? I'm talking about a feeling of tranquility, of stillness, of balance. Are you grounded? Do you feel as if your own, unique, internal compass is steady and true? Are you *centered*? Is this the life you want?

Where do you find peace?
For some people, that feeling of well-being comes on vacations, during baseball games, or after lots of sleep, yoga, and green tea.

Some pursue gardening or reading—activities that are calm and peaceful, giving them time to recharge and refocus. Others find their centers through a one-on-one relationship with a higher power or from being part of a congregation that shares common beliefs. What I believe is that we come into this world with a two-fold capacity: the ability to reason and a near-limitless potential for love. These are the benchmarks of our humanity and the criteria for the quality of our lives. So I believe inner calm comes from living a life of love and reason. In one way or another, most of us want to be good, giving people who make choices based on our values. When you are successful at that effort, you feel a sense of fulfillment. But what stands in the way of your achieving inner calm?

Dear Peter:

Do you know the story Thomas Merton told, recorded in his *Asian Journal*? I try to keep it in mind, much good as it does me. A Tibetan lama told it to him, and it's about a monastery of monks trying to escape from the Chinese when they invaded, and how one lama decided to drop all the monastery's goods and escape, while another stayed with the yaks, and the treasures, and was captured or killed. The moral, as Merton told it, was, "Do you want to be traveling with a train of yaks all your life?" Well, I always have, and the metaphorical beasts are getting to be too much of a burden to feed.

I've spent a great deal of my life seeking inner peace and calm. I've spent time in monasteries and on spiritual retreats, I've read a ton of books, meditated, explored yoga, and had endless late-

Quiz:
Do You Feel Balanced?

1. How do you feel when you wake up in the morning?
   a. Tired of the rat race.
   b. Pretty good—ready for a new day.
   c. Okay, so long as I get my coffee.

2. How often do you get quiet time to yourself?
   a. Never—there's too much I should be doing.
   b. Often—I always make time for solitude.
   c. Occasionally, but I don't really need it.

3. If and when you do take quiet time, can you actually relax?
   a. Not really—my head is always full of to-dos.
   b. Yes, if I really try to focus on being still.
   c. Kind of, but chances are I'll fall asleep.

4. Do you ever feel overwhelmed and suffocated, like it's all too much?
   a. Often.
   b. Not really.
   c. Sometimes.

5. Do you have a place—physical or internal—where you go to regroup?
   a. Yes—I have a retreat that works for me.
   b. I wish. I just don't have time.
   c. Not really, but I fantasize about getting away.

6. At the end of your life, what will you feel looking back on this period?
    a. Regret—I'm not living the life I want.
    b. Nostalgia—my life's pretty good right now.
    c. Mixed emotions—my life isn't perfect, but whose is?

7. Are you pleasant to be around?
    a. After a long vacation . . . maybe.
    b. I'd like to think so.
    c. If you catch me at a good moment.

8. Are you able to enjoy your vacations?
    a. Well, they're busy. My to-do list is almost as long on vacation as it is at home.
    b. Yes, I only wish I had more time off.
    c. About halfway through a vacation, I start to relax.

9. Given the choice, what would you pick:
    a. A thousand-dollar shopping spree at the store of my choice.
    b. A thousand-dollar vacation.
    c. A decluttering expert to help me rid three rooms of clutter.

10. If you were to paint a picture of your inner landscape, would it look like:
    a. The Scream by Munch.
    b. The Water-Lily Pond by Monet.
    c. Something in between.

Do you feel centered?

If your answers are mostly As:
Life is busy—cluttered—and it can be extremely hard to unwind, but still, you're missing every opportunity to do so. You don't take enough time to yourself. Even when you have a vacation it's go, go, go! Given the choice for a vacation or "stuff," you took the free stuff! As if that will improve your life! Having space to yourself is important. It's restorative. It's grounding. It gives you the chance to feel spiritually complete and fulfilled. You should know this by now. You can't blame your life for the lack of time and space. It's your responsibility to nourish your spirit. You will never find inner calm unless you actively search for it. We're about to discover how.

If your answers are mostly Bs:
Congratulations! You do a good job of preserving and protecting the time that you need for stillness and reflection, and the result is that you are, for the most part, grounded and true to your values. But keeping a hold on that inner calm always requires an active effort. In this chapter you'll find techniques to help you maintain and increase your sense of balance and core of strength.

If your answers are mostly Cs:
You struggle, as most of us do, with finding the right balance between the demands of a busy life and the need for inner reflection and fulfillment. It's hard to feel a sense of calm and well-being all the time, particularly if the physical and emotional clutter in parts of your life is overwhelming. Commit to clearing that clutter and you will clear your mind, gaining a sense of calm and well-being that will help you weather the ups and downs of daily life with aplomb.

night discussions with people who seem to have achieved a level of balance in their lives that I admire. I'm not a particularly religious person, but my inner spiritual life is fundamentally important to me.

Strangely, a great deal of clarity about my own "inner life" has come from the work I've done with families and their clutter. Without exception, all of the people that I work with—the people who struggle with clutter—have one thing in common: Somehow they have all lost their way in the jumble of things that they own. They've set out to create lives of happiness and meaning and yet somehow found themselves instead tied to a raft of stuff in an ocean that they have no idea how to navigate. Sometimes it's just a slight misstep off the path ("Those boxes of my deceased mother's things in the basement really stress me out, but I don't know where to start") and sometimes it's a total lost-in-the-dark experience ("There's so much stuff filling my house I feel totally paralyzed—it's destroying my life"). The stuff they own now owns and seemingly controls them. Worse still, for many of these people, their primary relationship is now with their stuff. The stuff takes over and fills not only the physical spaces of the home, but also the inner spaces of the person. It's interesting that we refer to what we own as our possessions when in many cases these things "possess" us and wield a power that feels impossible to exorcise.

If you read the sacred writings of any of the major religions, each contains repeated warnings about the danger of material goods. It's really interesting to me that these writings don't say not to own things—we all need things—but rather speak of the risks of placing the quantity of what we have before the quality and importance of our relationships. Distilled, it seems there's a consistent message: "If who we are and who we love doesn't come before what we have and what we buy, then there can be no balance or peace in our lives." For me, this is key to understanding what role the things we own come to play in our inner lives.

Remember those words we use when we talk of clutter: "suffocating" or "feeling buried" or "can't breathe." This is what clutter does, it sucks the life out of any space. Think of your immediate reaction when you walk into a cluttered space—anxiety, stress, feeling overwhelmed, or a strong wish to simply get away from it all. When clutter fills a space, there is no room for any light to occupy that space—literally and metaphorically. It is simply impossible to have a clean, centered inner space when your outer space is a chaotic, disorganized mess. Start with the physical clutter and then advance to those internal hurdles that are standing between you and inner peace.

Imagine the inner life you want

The first step toward clearing the clutter of your internal life— what I call spiritual clutter—is to clarify to yourself what your goals are. Here are some common goals to help you formulate your own.

- **A sense of purpose or mission**

Do you seek reason in your life? Maybe your religion or spiritual practice gives you a mission—be it to behave in a certain way, to help others, or to work toward salvation. Do you believe that no matter what happens, you have a set of core beliefs to comfort and sustain you in times of need?

- **A sense of completion**

Many people I talk to yearn for a sense of inner calm or completion. What helps you feel in touch with yourself? How would you describe the feeling of being complete? Do you wish you had more time for quiet, meditative reflection that left you feeling centered?

• Community

It may sound counterintuitive when you're talking about inner calm, but community can bring you a sense of having a place in the world. We are social beings by nature and gathering with others who seek what we seek and share in a similar belief system can be reassuring and strengthening for our inner lives.

• Decompression

Is there a place you go or something you do to regroup? It may be as simple as zoning out on your commute home, walking the dog, baking bread, having a drink, watching the news, playing with the kids, talking to your partner, or running around the block. You may notice that the days when you don't have time for your favorite escape are the ones when you feel more tired and overwhelmed. The answer may already be at hand. Don't underestimate the value of this sort of personal retreat. Give it the respect it deserves.

• Charity

Giving to others is a great way to get rid of physical and mental clutter. Just as donating belongings helps others while clearing out your home, donating your time has the unexpected side effect of clearing your sense of priorities and purpose. Organized religions often are pillars of charitable work. If you are looking for ways to serve your community, you may choose to do so through a religious body or volunteer group with a philosophy and mission that matches your own.

Activity
Define Your Vision for Your Inner Self

Stop, sit, and compose yourself for a few minutes. Relax, take a few deep breaths, and center yourself. Reflect on your current state of mind and sense of well-being. When your thoughts are clear and focused, complete the following table.

Describe your current state of mind:

Words that describe your ideal state of mind:

• _____

• _____

• _____

• _____

• _____

• _____

Describe your vision for achieving inner peace and calm:

What do you have to change if you want to achieve that vision?

Clear the clutter of unreal expectations

Most of us live our lives in a linear fashion, seeing each day as a series of tasks to be accomplished. But when it comes to finding a sense of truth and wholeness, everything gets a lot more abstract. You can't just pick something—like practicing yoga or painting in the garden on Sundays—and expect a sense of well-being to emerge. Fulfilling your spiritual goals isn't like attending jury duty, where you get credit just for showing up, no matter how grumpy you are about it. There's no free pass to a clear center. You need to take responsibility for yourself—for how you nourish yourself, for what you do and say, for the kind of person you are and the way you act toward others. Just as with the other parts of your life we have discussed, you have a responsibility and a commitment to actively pursue what will help you reach your spiritual goals.

Watch out for obstacles

Dear Peter:

I have a lot of mental clutter right now. I have not sought professional help yet because I can't afford it since I don't have insurance right now. I know I'm depressed. The cause for it is on the spiritual side of my life. From my first day of school in kindergarten, to my last day of high school before graduation I went to a private Christian school. Reading the Bible and having chapel and God was just a way of life at that school. It was something I just believed in, something I simply accepted as true and never questioned it. But now, I have had my chance to get out in the "real world" and have been on a roller-coaster ride ever since. I don't know what I believe in anymore. There are so many thoughts that go through my head every day, I don't know what to think. I don't want to be wrong and believe in something that isn't true, but I can't live the rest of my life this way. It's torture.

Too busy

You would like to devote more energy to your spiritual well-being, but you never seem to find the time. Ah, it's always the same excuse you've used before in other areas of your life. I hope you've come to realize by now that when you say you can't find the time, what you are really saying is: This is not a priority for me. You know and I know that how your time is spent every day is a series of choices and the only way to make room for a spiritual life is to move other time-sapping activities down on your list. What will you sacrifice? Is it time in front of the TV? Or is it time spent shopping for more stuff to crowd and complicate your life? Do you gossip on the phone? Work late every night? Consume hours surfing the Web? Spend several nights a week eating and/or drinking with friends? Are you more focused on buying gifts for birthdays and holidays than on celebrating the meaning at the core of the event? Do you feel that any alone time cuts into family time that you cherish? Where is the balance?

No life without food

We spoke earlier of the need for good food and appropriate choices in the nourishment of your body. Remember—you are what you eat. Our bodies are a reflection of the time we commit to them and the choices we make when we choose what we'll put into them. Good physical health comes from meals carefully chosen, lovingly prepared, and mindfully eaten. The nourishment of our inner life is no different. How are you choosing to feed your soul? Is it a commitment and a priority for you?

No foundation

Maybe you feel like something is missing—you yearn for a sense of completeness—but you have no idea where to begin. If you don't already gravitate to a certain way of finding calm—if you don't meditate or garden, or you've moved away from a place where you had a spiritual center—it can be hard to get started. What solo activities might work for you? Volunteering? Painting? Singing? Walking?

Disappointed

Maybe "disappointed" is an understatement. When life doesn't go as planned, when you suffer hardships, when loved ones die, it's easy to lose your way and find it hard to rediscover a spiritual calm and inner peace. But many of us know that these are the times when having a center, a faith, or a regular activity that grounds you is most important. It is often in these times that the "clutter" of our lives recedes into background and we are able to see clearly what is most important to us. A time of hardship can also be a time of great learning and insight.

Making it too complicated

Don't adopt an ideal for your spiritual life that you can't possibly fulfill. This isn't about becoming Job or Gandhi. This is about finding a calm, centered way of living that refreshes and restores you. When you can't live the way you think you should, you'll be tempted to abandon the whole effort. If you're trying to make more room for spirituality, increase your participation little by little until you reach a level that feels balanced.

Declutter your internal life

You can't find peace if you are in a constant state of chaos and clutter. It just can't happen! Your spiritual life is personal, and fulfillment takes infinite forms. I can't tell you what or how to practice,

Dear Peter,

Although my home is very organized and clear of physical clutter, my mental clutter is keeping me "stuck" in life. I am overwhelmed by information overload from the Internet. In trying to get my life "on track" in terms of personal growth and development, I find myself so overwhelmed by all of the information out there and the countless self-help gurus and life coaches, that I find myself paralyzed and fail to take action. I am always preparing to live (collecting information and organizing it), but never really living. So the mental clutter of information overload tremendously affects my sense of well-being, because I feel as though I'm "stuck" in life and frittering my time away.

Activity
What's Getting in the Way of My Sense of Well-Being?

Reviewing the sections above, write down the obstacles that stand in the way of achieving the inner life you seek.

• _____

• _____

• _____

but what I can tell you is that you have to establish and commit to your goals in this realm as in any other. Let's talk about how.

Strike a balance

Take a moment for a reality check. Look around your home. Think of how you spend your time. Is what occupies your spare time the meaningless clutter or a focus on what you value. Organization is not something that you *do*—it's where you are and how you live. You need to work to keep your focus on your core priorities— things that truly matter should occupy your time, your head, and your heart. If not, your internal clutter is not all that different from the stuff crowding your home.

Commit time

Being too busy is the biggest obstacle to calm. You may need time to clear your head and be quietly reflective. This requires carving out a regular time to "practice." Or you may find it easier and equally fulfilling to integrate spirituality into your everyday exis- tence by being generous and kind to others. The point is, you may never feel balanced unless you find a regular activity—and by reg- ular, I mean *every day*—that takes you out of yourself. Because one thing you can rely on is that if you spend all your time like a hamster on a wheel, you will never feel that life has meaning. You can't keep going and going and going. I firmly believe that every single person needs to pause at some point in the course of the day. For reflection, for rejuvenation, for perspective, for purpose. Surely you can see the logic of this! No matter what you choose as your peaceful interlude, you need to invest time and energy in order to yield returns.

Communicate

Connectedness doesn't happen in a void. You need to communicate with your community, with yourself, or even with a higher power, if you so believe. Usually when I ask you to communicate, we're working together looking for answers. We're trying to set goals and limits and to define exactly what you want from your life and how you plan to bring it to fruition. But spirituality is an abstract concept in which fulfillment generally comes from the process rather than the achievement of a specific goal. If you have young children, you might be hoping to set an example for them. If you want to include your family in your spiritual practice, I suggest you gather together and talk about each member's individual goals and how the family might coordinate efforts to meet them.

Set boundaries

When I help people establish boundaries in their homes, I take a very practical approach by reminding them that space is finite and that you can only have as much furniture as fits in your house. But there is a deeper reason for this. We need to understand our own limits and limitations as we go about our daily lives. Our decisions reflect how we choose to live in the world, where we direct our energies, and how we relate to others. This understanding of limits and the setting of boundaries is key not only to a balanced relationship with the physical world, but also to establishing and preserving your sense of calm and well-being.

Live by your moral code
I shouldn't have to say this, but I might as well make it clear from the start. Before you start meditating in front of a rock shrine or climbing Mount Ararat to question your god, you should already

Dear Peter:

Our finances are in tatters, our marriage is on its last legs, and neither of us really know how or where to proceed from here. There are a few things I do know for certain: I love my son beyond belief and everything I do, I do for his best; and that I can't continue living like this. I have this incredible urge now to not simply get rid of any extra material items, but also to get rid of mental clutter. I need to rid myself of my own negative thoughts and insecurities before reevaluating my life and determining exactly what I want. I am trying to focus on my own goals by first trying to figure out what those goals are. From there, I am ready to make my environment suitable to those goals—losing weight both physically and emotionally.

One thing I have discovered about myself is that I can't think or focus when things aren't organized, and when I can't think or focus, I lose track of me. The only thing I have to fight against, though, is my need to keep things so organized because my life in many ways feels out of control right now.

Thank you for putting in simple words everything that has been going through my head. Today I just began a journal because I realized that getting my thoughts out is part of my own mental self-organization. I also have a really bad memory so I am hoping journaling will help keep me focused on doing right by me and my son. If my husband decides to leave this marriage, I know I can't control that—what I can control, though, is making sure I am okay.

be living by your moral code. Honesty and integrity are core values to use in dealing with yourself and everyone in your life. Anything counter to these is clutter, just as real and destructive as the physical clutter that fills homes and destroys lives. If in any way, shape, or form you act in ways that you know or believe to be wrong, you need to stop. And if you have a serious problem—anything from a drinking problem to verbally abusing others—you need to get help to set things right. Are we clear?

Don't take on more than you can handle

When your life seems to overflow with responsibilities, I want you to reel it in. List the tasks that are crowding your brain. Prioritize them, decide what is reasonable to do, and get rid of the rest. Learning to set limits is easier said than done, but it's an important and powerful step to help you find balance in your life. Ellen has a full-time job, two young children with busy schedules, and an aging mother whose care and finances she also handles. On the surface, she manages to keep everything running smoothly, but inside she is overwhelmed and feels like she's sacrificing her own interests and needs. "I don't feel like a person anymore," she told me. "I'm an editor, a mother, a wife, and a daughter. I do all those jobs well. But I'm never just Ellen." Ellen couldn't afford to hire anyone to help either with her mother or with her kids, but something had to give. The answer came from her husband, Arty. He reminded her that every Sunday while he took the children to soccer practice, Ellen went grocery shopping. "Take that time to yourself," he told her. "We can shop together with the kids." Ellen committed to attend the same yoga class every Sunday afternoon. Additionally, she put a cap on the hours she was willing to volunteer at the library of her kids' school, and told her mother (who liked to call every day to find out the balance in her bank account) that they would only discuss her finances once a month. It wasn't much, but it reminded Ellen that she didn't have to say "yes" to all her loved ones' needs and requests. Establishing a limit of how much of her time she gave to others and setting clear boundaries between her needs and her family's needs fed directly into the health and well-being of Ellen's inner life.

Don't use overload as an excuse

Are you too busy to pay attention to your inner health? Really? After all we've been through together, you're trying to tell me that something is more important than your inner core of strength and balance? Isn't it obvious that if you're overwhelmed, scattered, and unfulfilled, then you can't possibly be your best self? And if you're not at your best, then you're all the more likely to feel like you have too much on your plate. It's a vicious circle. Clearing space—in your home and head and heart—will lead to better decisions. I've seen time and time again that great things happen in clear spaces—you just have to give the universe a little room to work its magic! It's up to you to make sure that space exists.

Make changes

If the life you live doesn't make you feel centered, then something needs to change. Let's explore how you can find a greater sense of balance and purpose as you go about your daily life.

Research and explore

Finding the right path to a sense of well-being can take real time and energy. Do you require physical stillness or activity to clear your mind? Would the right community—a group of people who share your values and goals—help ground you? You may have to approach this search the same way you'd look for a job. Start in your neighborhood, investigating groups that would be conve-

Dear Peter:

I have a cluttered mind, body, and spirit. Procrastination, feeling sometimes overwhelmed with all that I have to do, sometimes my mind just literally shuts down, leaving me feeling like I have no energy, feeling like a failure with all that I've not done, and it's immobilizing. I have unfinished business everywhere—regarding what I want to accomplish with my kids, a couple of new business ventures that I've been procrastinating on, working on decluttering my home, procrastinating on becoming healthier, a lack of focus at work, waiting till the last minute to buy gifts, and showing up late for dinner party reservations, ordering invitations late for a baby shower I'm helping to do, working on becoming more spiritual, and the list goes on and on.

I am a cluttered person inside but not always on the outside. To look at me, you'd never know. I'm just an average person, clothes and hair look neat, I'm very personable and get along with most anyone. But once someone gets to know me, I'm still all what you see but the layers beneath are a crazy, hectic maze.

I'm not giving up on me. I'm a work in progress. It's taking longer than I'd like (procrastinating like I do doesn't help), but something's got to give somewhere along the way to get me where I need to go. Thank you for your time, it was nice for the moment to get it off my chest.

nient for you. Ask friends and colleagues who seem to share your sensibility. Experiment with anything that sounds appealing and makes sense—from yoga to a silent retreat (except, obviously, illegal, mind-altering substances!). Read and listen to the words and music of people who might inform and inspire you. You can discover new forms of decompression at any age and time in your life. Don't expect a miracle the first time you try something new. Give it a chance. Remember: This is about finding what works for you.

Activity
Look for a New Escape

Write down five activities that you'd like to try.

Some suggestions: hiking or biking, subscribing to a classical music performance series, taking a pottery class, crafting, singing, keeping a journal, gardening, learning to bake bread from scratch, knitting, walking the dog, learning Tai Chi.

Activity	When you'll try it	How it made you feel

Small changes

Little by little, move your life in the direction of fulfillment. If you suddenly drop everything you ever cared about to pursue your spiritual center, people will accuse me of encouraging cults! On the contrary, I want you to value, respect, and preserve yourself as an individual. Feed your soul. Clear away activities that don't serve your goals—like shopping, accumulating more stuff, and watching TV—and give that time to activities that nourish your inner life.

Dear Peter:

Liz Gilbert, author of *Eat, Pray, Love*, said (on *Oprah* no less!) that (and I'm paraphrasing) if meditating is yet one more thing you *have* to do each day, don't do it. I think you can apply that concept to all areas of your lives (including spirituality) and streamline them down to the things that give us the most meaning and joy and enjoy them fully. One of my favorites is to combine my personal wishes and prayers for other people into my prayer bowl. It's a glass bowl with a small votive in the middle (the candle is encased in its own glass votive holder) surrounded by river stones. As I wish for something, or if I want to send healing energy or prayer to someone, I write the desire on a small slip of paper. I place it in the bowl (away from the candle) and light the candle nightly, meditating for a minute on positivity or healing or both. Once a month, I clean out the slips that no longer need prayer. For me, this consolidates many of my spiritual needs into one meaningful and enjoyable moment each day.

Accept imperfection

Remember that you're only human. You can strive for balance. You try to be a good person and to act with reason. But if you don't succeed 100 percent of the time, don't judge yourself too harshly. The whole point of your efforts is to grow and find strength. Seeing yourself as a failure only weakens and diminishes you.

Live in the present

Don't let your spiritual life take over your practical life

It may feel good to tune out of this world, but don't overdo it. Finding your bliss is one thing. Escapism is another. Even if you believe in an afterlife and want to devote your life to securing a prime parking spot in heaven, you shouldn't do it at the expense of being present here on earth. This life has meaning, and it's your responsibility to live in the here and now. Use your time here well. Remember my earlier comment about our capacity for love and ability to reason? How well do you measure against these? Relish your life. Respect others. Live by your creed. Find joy in being.

Face fears

Sometimes clearing our mind clutter and taking time for reflection is extremely hard. Slowing down, thinking things through, acting on your priorities—all this can force you to face some hard realities. You may have to admit that in some ways your life isn't going as planned? You may have to face ugly truths about your relationship with your partner or family or even yourself? Maybe old wounds that never healed will surface. I know it's hard. But I can tell you this: You can only live in denial for so long. There is nothing as liberating as being completely honest with yourself, confronting and overcoming your fears, and moving forward. You will feel lighter and clearer—uncluttered at last!

Dear Peter:

I've decided that I am not spending my entire life in a hot mess to regret that I didn't take the time to create the wonderful life God has given and graced me. I am taking off from work to create a home environment that my family and I will love. I am encouraged by the zones of clarity that I have created that my family and I love to spend time in. Just like you have to stop the cycle of domestic violence or family child abuse, I have chosen to stop the cycle of possessiveness, loneliness, greed, fear, and emptiness, and mental health issues that turn into self-destructive behaviors that feed hoarding, clutter, etc. Each time I clean out a drawer (I found $95 one day), I look at the closet and know I can tackle that project, too, or any bigger project!

Celebrate successes

I've spent untold hours, days, weeks, even months of my life helping people get rid of the clutter that has stood between them and their most authentic and rewarding life. I've opened mildewed boxes full of rotting old memories; I've seen towers of unused paper goods and closets stuffed with unworn clothing; I've confronted entire rooms full to the ceiling with God-knows-what. But when it comes down to it, what I really see in those homes is people who are burying themselves alive, chasing a promise that their things can never fulfill, and searching in the wrong place for a sense of joy, happiness, peace, and calm. For a myriad of reasons, these are people who want to build walls and fill holes and hide, hide, hide from themselves and the world. And when I help clear the clutter, what I am really doing is helping people face the truth and allow light to fill their homes and their hearts. That truth isn't about organizing bins and making room in file cabinets. It's about who you are, how you want to live your life, and how you can discover and nurture your best self. When the clutter is clear you open your space to blessings and opportunities you can't imagine—I've seen it happen time and time again. You can follow my recommendations and clear up every part of your life, but ultimately, you are the only one who can say that yes, you've done it. You feel tranquil, but energized. You've taken control and assumed responsibility. You're living by your priorities and feel a deep sense of happiness, having made real the vision you had for the life you wanted. Your life is in order. Well done!

Afterword

This book begins with the epigraph "Barn's burnt down—now I can see the moon." A reader e-mailed this bit of ancient wisdom to me and it stayed in my head for a long time. I like the notion that letting go of something, losing something as seemingly important as a barn, clears the way for a vision of something unexpected and beautiful: the moon. It says that in disaster there is hope; in loss, there is gain; in destruction, there is beauty. But I don't want you to walk away from this book feeling like sacrifice is the only route to change. I certainly don't want any good, hardworking farmers out there to burn down their barns. What I do want for you is the time and space and clarity that may come with an open mind—only then are you likely to see the moon. Life piles up. As the years go by, the heap of life gets taller and messier and it becomes harder to see clearly. And you forget all about that big, round harvest moon hanging up there in the sky. So don't burn down the barn, but do take the time to sort through your life, to clear the clutter, to actively make space for your hopes, dreams, and ambitions. Make space for love, for family, for work that inspires you, for a healthy body, spirit, and life. If you don't clear room to walk, you'll never find the path to your dreams.

Acknowledgments

Clearing the clutter from a home or any personal space is always a challenge, as we all know! Wading through the clutter that fills our heads is a whole different thing. Getting the words from my head to the printed page has always been a hugely collaborative process for me and—as usual—there are a ton of people without whom this book would never have seen the light of day.

To Ken—my life partner, best friend, and greatest supporter. It's fair to say that this book is as much his as it is mine. So many of my opinions and so much of my thinking is tempered by his wit and wisdom. One word seems puny, but it says it all: Thanks!

Families come in different forms and I've been lucky to have a few. First and foremost, my family in Australia. I'm sure they'll recognize themselves on a few pages of this book. I love them and I miss them—it's just a shame that it takes so long to get across the Pacific.

To all those who have helped and supported me in my fifteen years in the United States—thanks also. Especially to Holley and

Bob Agulnek and their extended family. We've been welcomed with open arms into their crazy clan and love every minute of it.

To the team at Paradigm and especially my book agent, Lydia Wills. I can't imagine there's a smarter one than her around. Insightful, talented, good-humored, and with an excellent knowledge of midcentury design and New York restaurants—who could ask for more?

To my colleagues and friends at Simon & Schuster/Free Press. From the hardest-working publicist in the country, Jill Browning, to the greatest editor, Suzanne Donahue, they have it all. My one regret is that I still haven't managed to declutter all those shoes from under an undisclosed desk in the editorial offices! To Carisa Hays and Martha Levin, thank you also. It's great to be associated with such a professional and talented team.

My work with the team at Harpo in Chicago is also hugely rewarding. From the top to the bottom, they are a wonderful organization to work with and have supported and encouraged me to no end. Oprah, the staff at *The Oprah Winfrey Show*, my producers, everyone at *Oprah & Friends* radio, and the talented team at Oprah.com continue to show that great things are possible.

My special thanks go to Hilary Liftin, my collaborator and a remarkable wordsmith. Her gift with the written word is truly amazing and I am so grateful to have her on my team. This book owes so much to her.

To Michael Feldman, who—at the eleventh hour—helped with the title.

Finally there is you—the reader. Without your constant support, unbridled enthusiasm, endless e-mails and notes, and insightful feedback, I could never do what I do. I am fond of saying that people have an endless capacity to surprise—for that and so much more, thank you.

Index

boundaries (*cont.*)
  in sense of well-being, 262,
    264–65
  between work and home, 45, 47, 68,
    69, 75, 85–86
  in workplace, 101–2, 109
brokers, 192
budgets, 182–84, 194
Bureau of Labor Statistics, U.S., 87

calendars, 145
  for tax paperwork, 203–4
cancer, 238
capital gains taxes, 192–93
carbon monoxide detectors, 229
careers:
  changing, 95–99
  jobs vs., 67
cars, safety of, 229–30
cell phones, ICE number for, 231
centering, in sense of well-being, 247,
    251, 259
change, 8–10
  decluttering and, 4–5
  difficulty of, 52
  in family life, 144–46, 147–48, 154
  fear of, 28, 33, 76
  in financial life, 186–93, 206
  in healthy lifestyle, 226–27, 228–40,
    244
  in relationships, 33–34, 42, 49–50,
    51–52, 61
  sense of well-being and, 264,
    267–69
  in work life, 78–79, 102, 105, 109
charity:
  donating children's stuff to, 153
  sense of well-being and, 254
"checking in," in relationships, 42
children, 138–43
  age-appropriate behavior of, 143
  arguments with, 128
  attention needed by, 126–27, 131–32,
    147
  chores and, 146, 151–52
  clothes for, 196–97

communication with, 116, 119–20,
    127–28, 134–35, 141–42, 144, 149,
    154
  and family vision, 134–35
  food and, 142–43
  independence of, 120, 122, 126, 127,
    149–50
  instilling value of giving in, 153
  money and, 163–64
  needs of, 112, 116, 117–18
  and parental expectations, 138
  parents' relationship with, 123–24
  as participants in rule-making,
    134–35
  physical clutter and, 140–42, 151–54
  respectfulness of, 137–38
  rules and, 126, 134–35, 138–39
  social and intellectual growth of, 119
  stuff and, 136, 140–42, 152–53,
    196–97
  see also family life; parents
choices:
  change and, 10
  in shopping, 186
cholesterol, 102, 212, 227, 238
chores, children and, 146, 151–52
civility, in relationships, 41–42
cleaning, health and, 228
clothes, cutting cost of, 196–97
clutter, emotional, 26–27, 50, 55
  in arguments, 38
  in financial life, 163–64
  health and, 208–9
clutter, mental:
  change and, 4–5
  in family life, 110–17, 128–51
  in financial life, 155–61, 175–202
  healthy lifestyle and, 207–11, 219–43
  physical clutter vs., 1–8, 270–71
  in relationships, 11–16, 31–59
  and sense of well-being, 246–53, 259,
    261–71
  in work life, 62–66, 77–107
clutter, physical:
  children and, 140–42, 151–54
  fear and, 61, 103

financial life and, 155, 189, 191,
202–6
healthy lifestyle and, 243–45
mental clutter vs., 1–8, 270–71
in relationships, 12, 59–61
and sense of well-being, 246, 253,
270–71
stress and, 228
in work life, 79–81
see also stuff
comfort, health and, 212
commitment:
in relationships, 52–55
in work life, 93
see also time commitment
communication:
with children, 116, 119–20, 134–35,
141–42, 144, 149, 154
in financial life, 176, 178–82, 206
in healthy lifestyle, 223–24
honesty in, 40
nonjudgmental, 40
in relationships, 29–30, 34–45
in sense of well-being, 262
staying focused in, 83
stress and, 233
in work life, 73, 81–85, 105
community, 254, 265
companionship, 19
completion, sense of, 253–54
conflict, fear of, 38, 53, 57
consumerism, 155–56, 157, 170, 173
see also stuff
credit card debt, 156, 157, 187–89, 198
criticism, responding to, 82, 85

date nights, 33
debt:
"bad," 164, 165
credit card, 156, 157, 165, 187–89,
198
"good," 164–65
reducing of, 172–73, 187–89,
199–200
decluttering, *see* clutter, emotional;
clutter, mental; clutter, physical

decompression, space for, 237, 244, 254,
265, 267
desk:
organization of, 92
purging of, 79–80, 81
diabetes, 238
diets, dieting, 222, 239
see also weight problems
disability insurance, 174, 201, 232
disagreements, *see* arguments
disappointment, and sense of well-
being, 259
divorce, 51–52
documentation, of workplace
communication, 84
*Does This Clutter Make My Butt Look
Fat?* (Walsh), 198
double standards, 139
Dyson, Brian, 68

Eat, Pray, Love (Gilbert), 268
economy, consumerism as measure of,
155
electronics, cutting cost of, 197
e-mail, 89–91, 102, 109
emergencies, financial, 158, 166, 167,
174, 191, 200–201
emotional clutter, *see* clutter, emotional
entitlement, sense of, 141, 164, 165, 167,
170, 193–94
exercise, 212, 236–38
balancing regimen of, 221, 224–25
finding pleasurable activities for,
238
time commitment to, 216–17,
220–21, 238
exit interviews, 106
expectations:
in family life, 122–24
in financial life, 167, 170
healthy lifestyle and, 213, 215–16
parental, 138
in relationships, 20, 24, 46
in sense of well-being, 256–57
in work life, 72
eye contact, listening and, 35

About the Author

Part contractor, part therapist, Peter Walsh lives to conquer clutter and help people reorganize their personal spaces. As the organizational guru on the TLC hit show *Clean Sweep*, a regular guest on *The Oprah Winfrey Show*, or the voice of reason on his weekly national XM radio program, *The Peter Walsh Show*, Peter demonstrates that decluttering is the sure path to a richer, fuller life.

Peter holds a master's degree with a specialty in educational psychology, has worked internationally in corporate training and health promotion, and possesses a keen sense of humor that regularly gets him out of the toughest situations. When not leading those lost in clutter to a happier, less-stressed life, Peter divides his time between Los Angeles and Melbourne, Australia.